SELF-HYPNOSIS AND SUBLIMINAL TECHNOLOGY

ALSO BY ELDON TAYLOR

*CHANGE WITHOUT THINKING (3-DVD set)**

*CHOICES AND ILLUSIONS: How Did I Get Where I Am, and How Do I Get Where I Want to Be?**

EXCLUSIVELY FABRICATED ILLUSIONS

*I BELIEVE: When What You Believe Matters!**

JUST BE: A Little Cowboy Philosophy

LITTLE BLACK BOOK

*MIND PROGRAMMING: From Persuasion and Brainwashing to Self-Help and Practical Metaphysics**

SIMPLE THINGS AND SIMPLE THOUGHTS

SUBLIMINAL COMMUNICATION: Emperor's Clothes or Panacea?

SUBLIMINAL LEARNING: An Eclectic Approach

SUBLIMINAL TECHNOLOGY: Unlocking the Power of Your Own Mind

THINKING WITHOUT THINKING: Who's in Control of Your Mind?

*WHAT DOES THAT MEAN? Exploring Mind, Meaning and Mysteries**

*WHAT IF? The Challenge of Self-Realization**

WELLNESS: Just a State of Mind?

Plus hundreds of audio and video programs in multiple languages

*Available from Hay House

Please visit:

Hay House USA: **www.hayhouse.com®**
Hay House Australia: **www.hayhouse.com.au**
Hay House UK: **www.hayhouse.co.uk**
Hay House India: **www.hayhouse.co.in**

Praise for *Self-Hypnosis and Subliminal Technology*

"Don't wait another day to achieve your dreams and goals! Eldon Taylor's guide for self-hypnosis and subliminal messages will show you how to liberate the creative power of your mind to realize success, self-improvement, health, happiness, and well-being. Create your own program with Eldon's proven tools for easy use at home, on the road, anywhere!"

— **Rosemary Ellen Guiley,**
author of *Develop Your Miracle Mind Consciousness*

"Do you want to be manipulated by those who understand how your mind works? No! So read this book and gain confidence in using subliminal-learning strategies. They are powerful techniques for manifesting your highest potential. Dr. Eldon Taylor has made this technology very accessible. Kudos!"

— **Emma Bragdon, Ph.D.,** author of *Resources for Extraordinary Healing*

"While pioneering psychologist Sigmund Freud is said to have chiefly concerned himself with the negative and destructive habits of the subliminal self—"the rats and beetles in the cellarage," as Aldous Huxley referred to it—Frederic W. H. Myers, another pioneer of the subliminal, was more focused on the hidden or buried treasures ignored by Freud. Eldon Taylor continues in the tradition of Myers, searching below the threshold of consciousness for meaningful processes and powers that enrich our lives and give purpose to them."

— **Michael Tymn,** author of *The Afterlife Revealed, The Afterlife Explorers,* and *Transcending the Titanic*

"Eldon Taylor's penetrating approach to hypnosis and the mind skips the nonsense and gets to the bottom line of making your life better, right now. If you know what you want, feel ready for change, or sense there is a repeating cycle in the works, this is the workbook that can change your life."

— **Gillian Holloway, Ph.D.**, author of *The Complete Dream Book*

"For those who want the facts, and 'just the facts, ma'am,' Eldon Taylor's new book, ***Self-Hypnosis and Subliminal Technology,*** *is a gold mine. This treasure is filled with brief yet complete explanations of the means by which we can quantum leap through a lifetime's worth of mental and emotional debris with the latest technologies. In fact, Eldon, the world's leading authority on subliminal communication, actually includes instructions on both self-hypnosis and subliminal modalities you can custom fit to your needs to empower any area of your life. I've used his techniques for years, and believe me—they work! It's the best how-to book I've read in a very long time."*

— **Angelina Heart**, author, teacher,
and facilitator of the Twin Flame pathway

"The power of the mind, the power of thought, the power of our beliefs—in this wonderful book, Eldon Taylor will show you how to use your own mind to create a life of joy, abundance, and success. ***Self-Hypnosis and Subliminal Technology*** *documents the research done on the mind, how hypnosis works, why it works, and how to use self-hypnosis to build a strong mind and belief system. This book also goes on to give you the tools necessary to build a solid foundation for changing your own self-defeating DNA, social programming, and other negative thoughts that are preventing you from reaching your highest potential or inner savant. A must read for all those truly interested in creating a life that is fun, exciting, and filled with adventures of the spirit."*

— **Charles Lightwalker**, author of *Medical Intuition Handbook*
and founder of the Spokane Holistic Chamber of Commerce

"The future of self-care is now with this comprehensive guide for self-regulation and self-health. You owe it to yourself to learn and use the powerful tools Eldon provides in this impressive book."

— **C. Norman Shealy, M.D., Ph.D.**, author of *Energy Medicine*

"This new book by Eldon Taylor is truly a gripping read. Eldon brings his fascinating life experiences to bear in a genuinely inspiring and uplifting way. I think anyone with my professional interest will find this book very helpful."

— **Raymond Moody, M.D., Ph.D.**, author of *Life After Life*

"For more than three decades, as I studied the brain, unbeknownst to me, Eldon Taylor thoroughly studied the mind. Fortunately, I have had the privilege to meet Eldon and to read his wonderful books. In ***Self-Hypnosis and Subliminal Technology****, he explains the power of the mind/brain/matter connection and how we can fashion a few incredible tools for self-improvement. Every seeker's bookshelf should have this book!"*

— **John L. Turner, M.D.**, neurosurgeon and author of *Medicine, Miracles, & Manifestations*

"The future of self-care is here with this revolutionary guide for self-regulation and self-healing. You owe it to yourself to learn and use the powerful tools Eldon provides in this impressive book."

— C. Norman Shealy, M.D., Ph.D., author of *Energy Medicine*

"This new book by Eldon Taylor is truly a gripping read. Eldon brings his fascinating life experiences to bear in a genuinely inspiring and uplifting way. I think anyone with any professional interest will find this book very helpful."

— Raymond Moody, M.D., Ph.D., author of *Life After Life*

"For more than three decades, I've studied the brain, and devoted myself to the effort to more rigorously study the mind. For decades, I have had the privilege to meet Eldon and to read his wonderful books. In *Self-Hypnosis and Subliminal Technology*, he explains the power of the mind that is unique to our kind and how we can harness it. He provides tools for self-improvement. Every seeker's bookshelf should have this book."

— John L. Turner, M.D., neurosurgeon and author of *Memory, Miracles & Manifestation*

SELF-HYPNOSIS AND SUBLIMINAL TECHNOLOGY

A How-to Guide for Personal-Empowerment Tools You Can Use Anywhere!

ELDON TAYLOR

HAY HOUSE

HAY HOUSE INDIA
New Delhi • London • Sydney
Carlsbad, California • New York City

Published in the United States by: Hay House, Inc.: www.hayhouse.com® • ***Published in Australia by:*** Hay House Australia Pty. Ltd.: www.hayhouse.com.au • ***Published in the United Kingdom by:*** Hay House UK, Ltd.: www.hayhouse.co.uk • ***Published in India by:*** Hay House Publishers India: www.hayhouse.co.in

Eldon Taylor's editor: Patricia Pohl • *Cover design:* Jenny Richards
Interior design: Nick C. Welch • *Interior illustrations:* Jana Roberts

The author of this book does not dispense medical advice or prescribe the use of any technique as a form of treatment for physical, emotional, or medical problems without the advice of a physician, either directly or indirectly. The intent of the author is only to offer information of a general nature to help you in your quest for emotional and spiritual well-being. In the event you use any of the information in this book for yourself, which is your constitutional right, the author and the publisher assume no responsibility for your actions.

First Hay House India Edition 2024

ISBN: 978-81-19554-22-5

Printed at Repro India Limited

This workbook is dedicated to you and the absolutely awesome power that resides within you. May you discover the glory of your being and manifest it in all that you do!

CONTENTS

FOREWORD

The power of the mind has always fascinated me, and I've studied it for more than 35 years. Having examined it from every conceivable angle, I now have an understanding of its predispositions, its bias operations, its defense mechanisms, and various other psychological characteristics that give rise to our individuality, as well as the herd nature of our makeup, to use an Aristotelian term. I've learned how chemicals can influence everything from expressed personality to our connection with God. I'm very aware that certain areas of the brain govern aspects of our experience ranging from our values (morality) to our mystical experiences. However, in spite of all this, I am still left in awe of the power that resides in the mind.

What is consciousness? There are many theories and ideas passed about nowadays, but the bottom line remains—we still don't have a *definitive* answer. Some assert that consciousness (mind) is but an artifact of the brain—an organ-derived event or illusion. For others, it doesn't reside in the brain, but somewhere outside of the body like an oversoul, or from some physical perspective like *zero point* (the energy field thought by some to be the source of all information).

According to many, the subconscious is the seat of the soul. To others, it's the source of all that our conscious mind can know; and the conscious mind can only guess at what's contained in the subconscious.

My purpose here is not to debate the nature of consciousness or the mind, but rather to explore its use. I've found that during deep states of meditation and hypnosis, people will often enjoy some of the most profound experiences of their lives and often manifest amazing capabilities. In my 35-plus years of researching consciousness, I've concluded that the two best tools for accessing the mind and assisting it to perform at its best are hypnosis and subliminal communication. A great deal of work has been carried out in these two areas, and they have both been proven effective.

However, for me their real advantage comes from their flexibility and ease of use. Self-hypnosis can be carried out anywhere, at any time. It can be used to help you believe in a desired outcome, uncover information hidden by your subconscious, and access your higher self. Subliminal communication can also be used extensively and is perfect for replacing thoughts and ideas that don't serve you with those that do. With this tool, you don't even have to take time out to use the program—you can work on your self-improvement while going about your normal day-to-day routine.

This work exists for you, to empower you and to assist you in enjoying your best in your every endeavor. I know that by employing subliminal-learning and self-hypnosis technologies, you'll have a new power that comes from freeing yourself of all those self-imposed limitations, fears, and doubts. Plus, you'll unleash an awesomeness about yourself that will absolutely encourage you to dare to be all that you've dreamed of being and achieving!

INTRODUCTION

This workbook is designed only as a primer—and a special sort of primer at that. There are innumerable books on hypnosis, subliminal technology, and the power of the mind. Indeed, I've written several myself. This work, however, is different.

The saying goes, "A picture is worth a thousand words." As such, you may read book after book, only to come away with mere words. Now these words may portray a picture of possibilities in your mind, but it generally won't be experiential. The intention here is to provide the experience.

One of my favorite questions is, *How high is up?* My disposition is such that I'm forever seeking more information, more knowledge, and more insight. Thus the question has more relevance to me than purely as an academic inquiry. It's because of this that the following material will provide not only an introduction to hypnosis and subliminal-learning strategies and technologies, but also an idea of the possibilities on the horizon.

While I've spent the majority of my life working in this area, I'm still quite often taken aback by both the scientific discoveries and the development of applied technologies for liberating the genie within. I'm absolutely convinced that with the right mind-set, making the impossible possible becomes simple and easy. The tools and technologies in this book are designed to provide you with an entrance to the near-magical world of what most people think of as special mental abilities. Whether you employ the tools in this work for learning and memory, habit training, self-healing, or personal relationships is your choice. The fact is, you'll gain a new and deeper insight into yourself and access to the real power in your life—your mind!

Skills accumulate, and as you use the material I provide here and on my website for your private application, you'll discover that your mental abilities also improve over time. Be patient with yourself and allow the process to work. Remember that much is gained from repetition and little remains without it, whether you're learning algebra or lifting weights.

So I encourage you to tap into the nearly unlimited power within. Use the programs and allow their influence to accumulate. The audio exercises are not one-time deals! It isn't like listening to an audiobook that you simply either recommend or forget when you're through. No, this is a *course*. It's simple and straightforward, one that almost anyone can complete. It has been deliberately simplified so that you can experience the possibilities that lie dormant within you—without earning a Ph.D. in the process.

I wish you success, and I always welcome your feedback at **www.eldontaylor.com**.

To your best,
Eldon

PART I

THE DESIRE FOR CHANGE

CHAPTER ONE

Why Change Can Be Difficult

"All changes, even the most longed for, have their melancholy; for what we leave behind us is a part of ourselves; we must die to one life before we can enter another."

— Anatole France

Everyone I've ever met or interacted with, everyone I've ever listened to or whose work I've ever read—in fact, every single human being from my experience—has, at one time or another, desired to change something about themselves. For some, the longed-for change may involve getting a better job, losing weight, improving memory, accelerating learning abilities, or increasing charisma. Indeed, there are very few individuals who find nothing they wish to improve.

While most people find it exceedingly difficult, if not sometimes impossible, to create the changes they wish, there are some who do manage to alter various aspects of their behavior and beliefs successfully. The questions seem obvious: What does it take to realize our total potential? Why do we sometimes succeed, while at other times we find only disappointing results?

When it comes to personal development, there are a variety of so-called experts with as many solutions as there are problems. Nevertheless, all of these specialists suggest, if not state directly, that the real power in the human development schema is that of the subconscious mind—if for no other reason than our habits. If this is so, why then can't I just instruct my subconscious to think differently and produce the results I desire? The answer to this question is really twofold. The first part lies in truly defining the change that needs to be made; the second is in understanding how the subconscious mind accepts information and why this can create problems.

What Is Change?

What is change? The idea seems simple enough. To some, it's a thing, often thought of as something like a commodity. For example, we desire more prosperity. The evidence of our success is money. So change in this instance is money, right? No, money is only the outer symbol that represents the shift.

The agency of change is within each of us. It isn't a thing. For someone to become more prosperous, he must think in a different order or magnitude than someone who's content with just getting by. At least one element in his life strategy alters before the change takes place.

Competing Strategies

Let's say, for purposes of illustration, that our hypothetical individual who wishes to be more prosperous was also raised with the belief that money is the source of all evil. A subconscious strategy may therefore work to sabotage any effort he makes to achieve real monetary success. In other words, in this instance the ego perceives safety as avoiding evil—that is, money.

Our hypothetical person may believe, on the other hand, that only money matters. However, there could still be subconscious strategies that get in the way. For example, assume that this person seeks to build a large company but is afraid of public speaking. How will he build a large and successful organization without communicating? When will the fear (public speaking) strategy kick in and knock out the goal (large company) strategy? How will the two ideas compete?

Conflicting strategies exist in nearly everyone. They often underpin what psychologists call "cognitive dissonance," the conflict that arises from holding two incongruent beliefs. Indeed, opposing strategies also lie beneath much of what's called "sublimation," or the acting out of unacceptable fantasies in a socially acceptable way.

Change Means Giving Something Up

It's easy to see why change can be so difficult, especially when you add in the fact that it means giving something up. That something may be a counterproductive belief or a competing strategy, or it may be tangible, such as the fulfilling feeling that food holds for some. To most people, giving something up means replacing it with something else. The smoker wonders what will replace the cigarette—gum?

The giving up, like change itself, is only a thing in its outermost form. Quitting smoking isn't really about the cigarette, but rather the feelings associated with them. This may involve 10, 20, 30, or more conflicting and competing strategies all balled up in one outward behavior.

Whenever we give something up, we must also confront the so-called unknown. This often gives rise to feelings of uncertainty. Most of us are very uncomfortable when we can't predict our emotions or responses. Fear of the unknown then becomes another obstacle in the path of change.

The Subconscious Mind

The other challenge to creating real change in our lives lies in the subconscious mind. This part of us is basically indiscriminate in how it accepts information. The problem then is twofold: first, there are already years of uncritical acceptance in my mind; and second, I act in reliance upon this information.

All the statements that have ever been accepted are present in our subconscious minds, and for most of us that's negative programming. Some psychotherapists have used numbers that indicate that for every input of positive messaging there are 100 bits of negative!

How many times have we all said to ourselves things such as, *I can't do it,* or *It never works for me*? How many times has each of us heard statements such as, "You're not old enough," "You're stupid," "Money is the source of all evil," "Life is difficult and then you die," "Thank God it's Friday," "That will never work," and "You'll never amount to anything"?

Our Inner Programming Is Essentially Negative

Just for fun, I once started a list of statements that I'd heard or said to myself that created negative expectations. I quit when I realized that to complete the list would take more time and paper than I was willing to dedicate to such a nonsensical task. Still, the message was loud and clear: the language that was programming many of my beliefs was essentially negative! Think about it. Every day, advertisers tell us that we're deficient—we need this or that to be complete, and that's why we should consume their products.

The consequence of this negative programming has been likened to a computer. The bio-computer mind/brain has accepted negative input just like a calculator accepts negative numbers. Then you or I add a few positive numbers to the program total and somehow expect change.

Our Defense Mechanisms Often Defeat Our Purposes

The fact that we act in reliance upon the information accepted indiscriminately by our subconscious minds is a pervasive problem. This means that if negative messages have caused us pain or fear, then we adapt our behavior and beliefs around avoiding those circumstances and outcomes.

With this adaptation come choices. Most choices of this nature are deeply rooted in the subconscious. Our subliminal beliefs—those in the subconscious that arise from our desire to be accepted and to avoid pain, humiliation, and rejection—determine our actions. All behavior comes from choice, even if the decision is made at a subconscious level. What happens is that we build defense mechanisms in order to protect ourselves from former bad experiences and possible future rejection.

These defense mechanisms often defeat our own best interests. For many of us, our worst enemy is often ourselves. Ignorant of these dynamics, it's easy to see why more than 90 percent of the people who attend or participate in motivational gatherings or products are unsuccessful. The fact is that every time we tell ourselves something such as, *I am good!* the subconscious gives a thought to the conscious such as, *Really! Good at what?*

Even when the behavior we desire is something as simple as success in our workplace, these subliminal beliefs come into play. For example, when I ask a group of people how many of them would like to come up front and speak to the audience for five minutes on some topic I'll assign them, rarely does anyone volunteer. A common fear is that somehow they'll suffer deep embarrassment, humiliation, and more. But this same group of people will respond almost unanimously to the simple, straightforward question: Do you want to be successful in business? Their answer is always yes!

To succeed in business, one must learn to speak. If there's a deep abiding fear of public speaking and a desire to be successful, there are contradictory motives present in the psyche. Thus, when a person reaches a certain level of success, for some inexplicable reason everything crumbles. What may be viewed as outside circumstances is, in truth, inner conflict. In the instance of the fear of public speaking, the closer to success the individual gets, the more powerful the exertion by subconscious processes to eliminate the impending threat. Conflicting factors or mechanics of our own psyche often defeat our stated desires without our conscious awareness.

Resistance to Change

Change can quite simply produce resistance! This is the process of avoiding change. It can take many forms, such as procrastination, feelings of discomfort or irritation, self-sabotaging strategies, and even an attitude that communicates, *I really don't want it after all!* The simple fact is this: True change is never effortless and can take a great deal of commitment.

That being said, the purpose of this book is to teach you about two techniques that you can use anywhere, and which deal with the problems from their core.

The power of hypnosis and subliminal communication exists largely in their direct communication with the subconscious. The conscious mind is generally in abeyance during hypnosis, although our defense mechanisms can still play a significant role in the outcome. The advantage of subthreshold (subliminal) communication is that it bypasses conscious awareness. Unlike hypnosis, where attention and conscious assistance are often necessary, subliminal messages aren't attended to by the conscious mind in any necessary manner. Because of this, we can decide for ourselves how to "script" our subconscious mind with this technology.

You Can Rescript Your Inner Talk

Using hypnosis, then, it's possible to access the hidden recesses of the mind to discover the source of a conflict and its solutions. Hypnosis also allows us to "seed" the subconscious mind with thought patterns and ideas that can serve us as opposed to sabotage us. But for me, the most exciting use of hypnosis is for deepening meditation exercises and using this to access information from my higher self.

As for subliminal communication, it works by allowing the positive messages or affirmations to eventually overtake the negative information contained in the subconscious. This new data rescripts our inner talk, thereby priming positive self-beliefs, which begin the cycle of self-fulfilling prophecies. When this happens, the subliminal beliefs that formerly were self-limiting begin to change. As they change, so do we!

CHAPTER TWO

Exploring the Boundaries of the Mind

"Men are not prisoners of fate, but only prisoners of their own minds."

— Franklin D. Roosevelt

What is the limit to the power of the mind? For years the power of positive thinking has been heralded as almost a supreme power to attract and create wealth, power, relationships, success, and general prosperity of all kinds. Recently—at least within, say, the past 30 to 40 years—the power of the mind has also been championed as the body's great healer. Words and abbreviations have been added to our vocabulary to accommodate the exchange of ideas regarding this seemingly miraculous interface between mind and body, words such as *psychoneuroimmunology,* or PNI for short. More recently, several researchers have stepped forward to inform us that our thoughts, the stuff in our minds, engage and activate the DNA molecule, and for this labels such as novelty-numinosum-neurogenesis and psychosocial genomics have been added to our vocabulary.

Does Mind Power Have Limits?

Think of it: what is the limit of the mind? Is it possibly among our few remaining and largely unexplored frontiers? More important, what does novelty-numinosum-neurogenesis have to do with hypnosis or subliminal learning?

One of my icons is Ernest Lawrence Rossi, Ph.D. He is the recipient of three lifetime achievement awards for outstanding contributions to the field of psychotherapy from the Milton H. Erickson Foundation in 1980, the American Association of Psychotherapy in 2003, and the American Society of Clinical Hypnosis in 2008. He's also a Jungian analyst and the science editor of *Psychological Perspectives*. Rossi has shown that through the use of hypnosis, the modulation of activity-dependent gene expression can be manipulated. In his words:

> The molecular messengers generated by stress, injury, and disease can activate immediate early genes within stem cells so that they then signal the target genes required to synthesize the proteins that will transform (differentiate) stem cells into mature well-functioning tissues. Such activity-dependent gene function and its consequent activity-dependent neurogenesis and stem cell healing is proposed as the molecular-genomic-cellular basis of rehabilitative medicine, physical and occupational therapy as well as the many alternative and complementary approaches to mind-body healing.[1]

He also states:

> The therapeutic replaying of enriching life experiences that evoke the novelty-numinosum-neurogenesis effect during creative moments of art, music, dance, drama, humor, literature, poetry, and spirituality, as well as cultural rituals of life transitions . . . can optimize consciousness, personal relationships and healing . . . [2]

Rossi has shown that these life-enriching experiences can be replayed or even created in the mind, and they can evoke the novelty-numinosum-neurogenesis effect. However, he points out in an article published by *Annals of Psychotherapy & Integrative Health,* the official journal of the American Psychotherapy Association, "The dark side of the novelty-numinosum-neurogenesis effect is that it is very labile and vulnerable to conflict, trauma, stress, and outright manipulation by authoritarian social forces that seek to manipulate human belief systems and behavior."[3]

Our Organic Programming: Compliance

I discussed many ways that we're all manipulated or brainwashed to some degree every day in my book *Mind Programming.*[4] One of the most used methods involves activating an altered state of consciousness to program the subconscious. You'll learn all about altered states of consciousness later in this book, so for the moment, let me just point out that the same brain-wave state we associate with hypnosis, known as alpha, is the state we all go into when we watch television. The fact is that the average person will slip into alpha within minutes, and many will in a matter of seconds.[5] This is a state of hyper-suggestibility, and therefore we're prone to accept suggestions to buy products and believe in certain ideas.

So as it turns out, most of us have been deliberately programmed without our knowledge for our entire life—at least to some extent. It also doesn't help that our own psychology can be used against us. I see this most clearly in the principles of compliance. I cover this issue in depth in *Mind Programming,* but basically there are 11 principles of compliance, which are character traits, desires, and needs that allow others to manipulate us.

1. Social beliefs: These are among our strongest personal beliefs and often conflict with individual desires. We're basically told what's acceptable and what isn't; and being herd animals, we simply follow along.

2. Reciprocity: Studies have shown that the act of gift giving produces the need to reciprocate. From a warm handshake to inside information, a favor extended implies a gift in return. Persuasion, compliance, and negotiation expert Dr. Robert Cialdini calls it "the old give and take and take and . . ."[6]

3. Social proof: Merchants list testimony after testimony from faithful, satisfied users to sell us their wares. What many agree to must be true, good, and desirable. But remember, not so long ago, everyone believed the Earth was flat!

4. Association: This is the effort to link favorable feelings with a product or aim. We see politicians with apple pie, babies, and the American flag. We see stunning men and women in the most unlikely of places, with the most unlikely of apparel, just to connect the product with these images. Similarly, television producers use canned laughter to punctuate comedy. Many people don't actively notice this, for in our culture, we often overlook sound. Don't discount even the most innocent of features that accompany a product or advertisement. The companies behind them spend billions annually on deliberately applying skillful knowledge to manipulate you.

5. Conditioning and association: As with the associations intentionally built into most advertising, certain consciously undetected associations can operate on existing conditioning and pair with it to produce new conditioning.

6. Liking: The more we identify with others and feel comfortable with them—the more we like people—the more often we comply with their requests. Discussing anything so obvious may seem ridiculous, but the liking principle has nuances unfamiliar to most of us, such as its mechanical features. This means, for example, that if a smiley face is paired with a country's flag, we'll be predisposed to like that country.

7. Authority: "Authority, authority, authority" has a ring to it similar to the secret of retail success: "Location, location, location!" Everywhere we turn today, the authority instructs, informs, and becomes that which we come to trust with our very lives. How did we survive before we had so many different experts?

Everything in the world is sold partly on the basis of authority. We must rely on this sometimes in our high-tech society, yet blind reliance is absolute ignorance. Fortunately, more and more people have become suspicious of authorities. More important, modern technology makes it possible for any of us to check on information and experts much more rapidly.

8. Scarcity: "This is the last one; better take it. Act now, limited quantity. Don't delay. Don't miss out. Time is limited. Sale ends today. Hurry—first come, first served." These are but a few of the scarcity statements we find in advertisements for everything from pickles to panty hose. Why does the compliance principle of scarcity drive us? In a word, *greed!*

9. Drives: These are the basic built-in needs of the species. In psychology, human drives, or forces, are often referred to as the 4 F's: fight, flight, feeding, and fornication. I tend to think that these have evolved with the advent of modern merchandising and deferred payment. Consequently, my view incorporates 5 F's. What is the fifth force? Simple: *More!* No one has enough; everyone wants more. Gain has somehow become desirable in itself. Today the word *more* equals power, prestige, status, and peace of mind. It now means quality as much as quantity: "Keep up with the Joneses!"

10. Justification: Extenuating circumstances can justify radical actions. Indeed, a tenet of our jurisprudence system allows for this, which is why there are rulings such as self-defense, justifiable homicide, and the like. This principle is probably the most often overlooked tool of compliance. An excellent example of its power exists in a classic television commercial. The viewer sees a woman performing the many tasks of an absolutely frantic day: shopping, cleaning, caring for children, banking, and so forth. At the end of the day, she (a very beautiful and seductive woman) relaxes in her bath, covered by foam. The spot advertises a bubble bath and ends with the statement, "Let XYZ product take you away." It's an excellent commercial that employs more than one compliance principle. Still, it's the notion of justifying indulgence that makes it so powerful. How else do you sell bath bubbles?

11. Informed compliance: Being informed doesn't necessarily remove us from the power of these principles. They obtain most of their power because they operate automatically, not from thinking a matter over. Cialdini refers to the response as "click, whirr."[7] He and other social scientists regard this automaticity as necessary. Normally we benefit from sticking with people we like, who have done favors for us, and who have authority. What would happen if we simply reversed all these patterns?

In *Mind Programming,* I also showed how much manipulation goes on in our media and on behalf of almost everyone who has a product or a sound bite he or she wants us to believe. Bottom line, when we know the abuses already present, it's easy to begin to think that we live under a "media-ocracy."

The best defense is knowledge. I've also learned that the best way out of programming is reprogramming. The two most effective techniques I've found for this are hypnosis and subliminal communication, and that's what I intend to teach you in this book. However, let's first continue looking at other factors that exert control over our lives.

Personality

Personality also plays a significant role in what you can expect to experience in life and, in particular, your degree of sickness or health. Medical professionals often deal with personality as experimental scientists deal with random variables; and without the natural differences, such terms as *normal* or *pathological* have no meaning. The variable we call *personality* is the essence of the human condition. In fact, it extends beyond the human sphere into at least the animal kingdom.

But does personality have anything to do with illness? A number of cases clearly demonstrate that it can influence the manifestation of disease. This is so well documented that specific personality types have gained recognition as leading candidates for each of the seven psychosomatic ailments: peptic ulcers, ulcerative colitis, hypertension, hyperthyroidism, rheumatoid arthritis, neurodermatitis, and asthma.[8]

Multiple-personality patients routinely devastate mechanistic beliefs about the body. A patient may test totally normal in every physiological sense, but with a shift of personality, some as quick as the snap of a finger, the individual may exhibit hypoglycemia or even diabetes.[9] How does a personality shift alter body chemistry in seconds? Can a personal belief system, such as "who I am," alter cellular behavior instantly?

Dr. Frank Putnam of the National Institutes of Health (NIH) studied how people with multiple personality disorder go from one personality to another. He found that their electroencephalograms (EEGs) "change as dramatically as though the electrodes have been taken off one person and placed on another." Other such patients have demonstrated everything from eye-color change to having one menstruation cycle per month for every personality housed within the patient.[10]

A change in personality can cause an instant transformation in the way that cells behave. What mechanism allows for such a dramatic shift in a person's blood chemistry? What trigger exists to make this possible?

In another instance of the mind influencing the body, Madelaine Visintaines of the University of Pennsylvania has linked helplessness to cancer. She concluded that this quality is somehow taken by the body to mean an absence of "the ability of the organism to resist tumor development."[11]

Researchers at Duke University showed hostility and mistrust to be key predictors of heart disease and early death.[12] H. J. Eysenck summarized a group of European studies and found the following:

1. Individuals who tended to repress their emotions in the face of stress were far likelier than others to die of cancer.
2. Those who rated high on emotional frustration and aggression had a high rate of cardiac-related death.
3. Personality variables were more predictive than smoking in the occurrence of lung cancer. For example, smoking was virtually a prerequisite for getting lung cancer, but of the smokers, only the emotionally repressive types seemed to contract the disease.[13]

There's further evidence that personality ties in with clusters of diseases. At Georgia State University, researchers discovered that people with eating and drinking disorders also suffered depression, indecision, chronic fatigue, low self-esteem, physical weakness, and hopelessness.[14] At the University of Texas–Austin, higher cancer rates occurred in under-stimulated mice and mice with minimal expressive behavior.[15]

Karl Goodkin of Stanford University's School of Medicine reviewed studies of women prone to cervical cancer. He created this composite personality type that he suggests is at higher risk for cancer:

1. Overly cooperative
2. Extremely self-sacrificing
3. Overly optimistic to the extent that they are in a state of denial of reality
4. Sociable to a fault

However, women who developed cervical cancer had these traits as well:

1. Tended to be hostile
2. Fearless
3. Hardheaded
4. Punitive toward others
5. Blunt in social situations[16]

What have we discovered from these pathogenic personality models? Nearly every type or characteristic has appeared. However, you need not fear that "personality kills." Notice the qualifiers of excess: overly cooperative; not altruistic, but extremely self-sacrificing; hostile rather than assertive; fearless instead of brave. Traditional cultures always associate health with balance. We may catch up with that tradition.

We've already recorded personality profiles characteristic of many illnesses.[17] This might already serve to predict disease-prone or at-risk persons. Researchers have linked precursors to many illnesses: mononucleosis to stress in school; herpes to loneliness; positive mood, hope, and social support to cancer survival; tough-mindedness and a will to live with AIDS survival.

Stress

Hans Selye introduced stress as a factor effecting health. "Selye's lifetime of ground breaking research culminated in a theory of how mental and/or physical stress is transduced into psychosomatic problems by hormones of the hypothalamic-pituitary-adrenal axis of the endocrine system. Scharrers and Harris confirmed and expanded Selye's work. They gave us the discovery that, 'secretory cells within the hypothalamus could convert neural impulses that encoded mind into the hormonal messenger molecules of the endocrine system that regulated body.'"[18]

Sheldon Cohen of Carnegie Mellon University in Pittsburgh reported a study that links emotional stress to the common cold. "Cohen's group found that the rates of respiratory infection and colds increased in accordance with stress levels reported on questionnaires . . . The (stress) pattern held despite statistical controls for various influences on immune function, including age, sex, education, allergies, weight, viral status prior to the study, cigarettes and alcohol, exercise, diet, quality of sleep, number of housemates, and housemate infection rates. The link between stress and colds also proved to be true independent of the personality characteristics assessed by questionnaires." [19]

Life's various circumstances connect with wellness. A researcher at The Ohio State University reported that marital stress weakened the immune response.[20] George Solomon of UCLA originated the concept of psychoneuroimmunology. He also reports that the stress and strain of life crisis "states" diminished the immune response.[21] Ted Melnechuk, director of research communications for the Institute for the Advancement of Health, adds the following observations:

1. Men married to dying women have a lowered immune response.
2. Monkeys separated from their mothers experience immune suppression.
3. Visual imagery has been shown to decrease tumor growth.

4. Nerve signals have been shown to travel from the brain to the thymus and back to the brain, demonstrating a two-way communication with this important relay station for immune substances.[22]

Dr. Henry Bennett at the University of California Medical School at Davis believes that he can demonstrate the connection of the biochemical stress hormones (epinephrine, norepinephrine, and vasopressin) to more than just the immune system. He has cited evidence that these hormones have something to do with consolidating memories.[23] Remember this one, because I believe that, added to our other data, it will become more significant.

What Happens When You Reverse Some of These Patterns?

Some years back, cosmetic surgeon Dr. Robert Youngblood employed a subliminal audio program that I made to lower stress and anxiety in patients about to undergo surgical operations. We hypothesized that lowering patient stress, anxiety, and associated feelings would reduce anesthetic requirements. He examined the records of 360 patients who'd undergone the same or similar surgical procedures to determine total anesthetic usage, and our hypothesis proved valid.

He applied the audio program during pre- and postoperative procedures and throughout surgery. The overall anesthetic requirement declined by 32 percent in the patient group that received the subliminal program. Thus, group B, the experimental group, which also consisted of 360 patients, required almost 1/3 less medication (anesthetic) than group A, the historical control group. On analysis, another result emerged. The postsecondary care requirement also substantially declined.[24]

We went on to conduct a study at a medical facility in Nevada that offers a number of different high-tech procedures, including magnetic resonance imaging (MRI). This test allows 3-D pictures of the inside of the body, including soft tissue; no other test offers the information that it can provide. MRI requires that the subject be "loaded down a skid into a chamber," in the words of one of the techs. They have to put patients slowly through a long, very narrow, complicated metal tube. Inevitably, some patients fear closed-in places. In addition, most have some anxiety about the sheer quantity of machinery, the sterile surroundings, the kinds of tests they're undergoing, medical care in general, and hospitals in particular. A CAT scan only requires that the patient go through a ring, but some need sedation even for that.

The medical facility asked us to create an audio program that would ameliorate these conditions. We employed a combination of special frequencies designed to entrain (or pace) the brain while stimulating certain effects, and we added subliminal messages and guided imagery. The chief CT technician reported a complete elimination of phobic responses when the audio program was used.[25]

The mind, the brain, the mind/brain was again altering physical and emotional experiences. While in Nevada, I learned that many hypnotists in the state apply hypnosis for breast enlargement. Indeed, the research clearly shows that hypnosis can be used to enlarge breasts. In 1971, Peter Mutke, M.D., reporting his results to the department of neuropsychiatry at UCLA, showed for the first time how this could be done.[26] Since then, several scientific studies have replicated this finding. Following the pioneering work of Mutke, I developed a subliminal InnerTalk® program to test its effectiveness at breast augmentation. In one clinical study carried out in the UK and published in *What Medicine*, women reported approximately 2 cm of breast growth and a fuller cup size within 30 days.[27] Where are the boundaries? Where should we make them? What else is the mind/brain capable of?

Exploring the Far Reaches of Mind Power

Exploring the mind and pushing its capabilities so that it works for us, as opposed to against us, has long been my passion. I decided long ago that "believing in yourself always matters," and I covered much of the reasoning behind this in my book *I Believe: When What You Believe Matters!*[28] However, while the purpose of this book is to teach you tools you can use rather than provide you with a treatise on the mind, I do think it's important to have at least a basic understanding so that you have some idea of what's possible. Here are just a few highlights of the facts and findings I shared in *I Believe,* a few of which we have already touched upon, but they're worth repeating:

1. As we've just seen, the mind and beliefs can influence our DNA.[29]

2. Belief can also deliver the strangest of maladies, complete with physical symptoms. Indeed, in some instances of mass hysteria, an entire group has fallen ill with the same symptoms, such as a rash, high temperature, or abnormal blood counts. In one such instance of mass psychogenic illness, several people reported symptoms that included dizziness, muscle cramps, tremors, and shortness of breath. This occurred in Beirut at a time when the city was under near constant threat of violence, and the case was reported to the Saint George Hospital University Medical Center, where the attending health-care professionals finally diagnosed the problem as "mass psychogenic illness (epidemic sociogenic attacks)."[30]

3. There are documented multiple-personality cases where the subject has normal blood sugar in one personality, and in the instant that another personality takes over, the subject will test hypoglycemic. As if that isn't enough to ponder, consider this: There are cases in which eye color changes with the personality, and ones in which extreme allergies come and go with the switches.[31]

4. The power of your intention (thoughts) has a well-documented influence on random-number and random-event generators. According to Dean Radin's *Entangled Minds,* the calculated odds that the

effects observed in these studies were random or chances are 1 in 10^{76} (1 followed by 76 zeros). Thoughts influence machines![32]

5. Remote viewing, the power of the mind to see things at a distance, has been well studied. Ingo Swann, working with the Stanford Research Institute in California, particularly with researchers Russell Targ and Harold Puthoff as chronicled in their book *Mind-Reach,* initiated a multimillion-dollar government project that lasted years, investigating the influence of mind on matter and the possibilities of employing remote viewing as a spy tool.[33]

One of Swann's most impressive feats occurred during a study where they looked at the possibility that he could influence the output of a magnetometer (a device that detects and measures the magnetic field, detecting the tiniest vibrations of subatomic particles while screening out the strong vibrations from the most common electromagnetic fields) using just his mind. Not only was Swann successful at affecting the output of the machine, he also projected his mind into the apparatus to see what the insides were like. He was basically able to draw the insides of the machine, something that hadn't been published anywhere, even though the magnetometer's "internal parts were shielded in alternating layers of aluminum, copper, nobium[*sic*], and other metals to block electromagnetic and other kinds of fields, and it was then encased in concrete five feet below the lab floor. There was no way for Swann to actually see or interact with the device."[34]

6. Mind/consciousness has also been shown to influence plants. Cleve Backster, a fellow former lie-detection examiner, showed not only that plants respond to human consciousness and actions, but also that they have memory. Backster claimed to be able to measure the influence of consciousness on white blood cells, eggs, and yogurt cultures.[35] Harold E. Puthoff and Randall Fontes at the Stanford Research Institute published a paper that supports Backster's view of consciousness in a report called "Organic Biofield Sensor."[36]

Randall Fontes's career path was largely set by his graduate project, in which he sought to research the action potential in the algae Nitella to determine sensitivity to various external stimuli. His conclusions clearly demonstrate a reaction or exchange of some kind that takes place between plant and human consciousness, and his research was highlighted in the best-selling book *The Secret Life of Plants,* by Peter Tompkins and Christopher Bird.[37]

7. Mind has been shown to exert effects over a distance. In my book *Wellness: Just a State of Mind?* I reported on how some cells were removed from the body and then divided between two petri dishes. One dish was taken as many as five miles away from the other, yet when an electrical shock was delivered to one set of cells, the other

set responded as though they'd just received the direct current.[38] Cell consciousness was communicating at a distance.

8. Trained meditators control many aspects of their bodily functions. Dr. Herbert Benson of Harvard Medical School has reported on Tibetan monks who can produce enough body heat to dry wet sheets placed on their shoulders in a cold, damp room. According to the *Harvard Gazette,* this type of temperature control is common among trained meditators.[39]

The Other 90 Percent?

As you can see, the mind has repeatedly been shown to have abilities beyond the merely mechanical. There are those who would like to say this is because most of us only use about 10 percent of our brains, and that it's the other 90 percent that holds this supreme potential. Well, the truth is that no such measurements have ever been made. However, this is a powerful metaphor for looking at limitation. Savants have demonstrated amazing abilities in certain areas, such as telling you on what day of the week your birthday will fall 50 years hence even before you can finish your sentence. So the question is: Can we find our own inner savant? Could we all have such skills if we only believed that we could? Could we at least train this ability within ourselves if we believed the endeavor would be successful?

In contrast to all the marvelous potential we might conjure up, there are also many sinister possibilities. In my book *Mind Programming,* I cited the conclusion reached by the U.S. Central Intelligence Agency regarding brainwashing, as reported to Congress by Jules Romains, which stated flatly that a man could be persuaded to kill his aged parents and cook them in a stew.[40]

What then is the real power of the mind and the engine that appears to drive its most spectacular possibilities? In a word: *belief!* In my view, this is the ultimate frontier. One day, perhaps we'll have the switch that turns on belief, and we'll be able to trigger within ourselves a cure for cancer just as easily as flipping on a light. Or maybe we'll want to experience being lighter than air, so we'll engage yet another switch, and voilà, we'll be able to levitate.

The Power of Mind and Its Vested Belief

This is what I hold to be true: belief dictates your life as surely as magnetism directs a compass needle. If you deem yourself unworthy, you'll prove it to be so. If you think you're unfit, you'll find a way to manifest that. I can't overemphasize the potential power in our beliefs and the necessity of choosing them wisely.

Unfortunately, most of us haven't consciously chosen the bulk of our beliefs. In my book *What If?* I made the case for examining your life and all that you hold true.[41] As Socrates is credited with saying, "The unexamined life is not worth living." I believe that you have both the prerogative and the obligation to know what you think and why. Those who choose to close their minds, believing that they know all there is to know, that they have the only right way, or that there's no such thing as *blank* (say, miracles), have blinded themselves to experiencing much of the true meaning in life—and of being who they really are.

It's popular in certain circles today to believe that science has all the answers. This is interesting, especially when those who make this claim often fail at being true scientists—fail by definition, for a scientist is someone who investigates, not someone who closes the mind and refuses to look. *Skeptic* is another word often heard nowadays to describe those who banish the possibility of life being more than just what's currently provable. This, too, is a misnomer, for the word implies openness to inquiry. History informs us that true skeptics eventually find that nothing is certain, including science. Epistemological certainty simply doesn't exist, except for uncertainty—and that can't be known for sure.

What Do You Believe?

So what is it you believe? Those tenets can empower your life or cripple your every hope and ambition. The good news is that the tools you'll acquire from this workbook and the accompanying audio and video material, both on the audio download and from my website, will empower you to choose the programming that serves your highest aspirations. I hope you remember to use it often, for I know you absolutely possess an awesome power within!

Part II

HYPNOSIS

CHAPTER THREE

Hypnosis: A Brief History

"The eye sees only what the mind is prepared to comprehend."

— Henri Bergson

In 1765, Franz Anton Mesmer employed magnets to produce miraculous cures. Later, most critics said that Mesmer obtained results due to the power of suggestion in what James Braid, a Scottish physician and surgeon, termed *hypnosis*.[1] That term persisted despite Braid's attempt to alter it.

The word originated from the observation that subjects under the influence of Mesmer seemed to enter a state of "nervous sleep." Later Braid decided that the term *monoideism* more appropriately described this state. A single idea, held to the exclusion of others, produced the phenomenon demonstrated by Mesmer. Others also used imagination and imitation to produce an altered state of consciousness, and so healed the chronically ill. Braid discounted the magnets entirely.

History twists. Science plays with opinions. We've come the better part of the way to admitting that hypnosis *and* magnets contributed to the miracles of Mesmer's time. For years Mesmer and his followers cured patients of a host of different illnesses using his methods. In time, Mesmer suffered disgrace, and he died in obscurity. His fall from favor stemmed in part from the scientific community's inability to replicate his work. They maintained that the magnets in and of themselves didn't work. But something worked. People could see again; they could walk again.

Why do we often overlook cures in favor of indictments? In believing that it was magnets rather than the power of suggestion that effected the cures, Mesmer had it wrong. But by and large, the ill who had been cured, remained cured. Many factors tangled together here. Even referring to both hypnosis and magnetism is an oversimplification. The fact remains: something totally out of the ordinary, mechanical, body-part models worked. Braid settled on the power of suggestion, or *hypnosis*. Hypnosis has demonstrated results for asthma, hypertension, bleeding, dermatitis, various emotional disorders, speeding the rate of healing, and much more.[2] Is this a matter of words having curative powers?

Hypnosis to Cure Hysterical Paralysis

In the 1880s, Jean Martin Charcot regularly demonstrated one of his favorite hypnotic procedures to medical personnel at the Salpetriere hospital in France. He would hypnotize patients suffering from hysterical paralysis; and in that state, they would stand and walk on Charcot's command. In ordinary consciousness, the same person would "crumple to the ground."[3] Did the suggestions given during hypnosis revivify a cellular memory of wellness? Did they remove or circumvent psychological barriers that sustained the dysfunction? Sigmund Freud theorized that "emotions not expressed in words or actions would find expression in some sort of physical ailment."[4] Did hypnosis alter such unexpressed feelings?

The Information Exchange

Physicists have often reported the role of the observer in influencing the outcome of physical measurement and observation. Indeed, many physicists believe that consciousness interacts with matter. Studies employing sophisticated statistical measurements support evidence for mind-matter interaction.[5]

Belief in ourselves, our abilities and powers, and our influence over our own lives and the world around us, is at the crux of what each and every one of us experiences in life. Belief may define and delimit our every experience. Eroding our faith is doubt. Self-doubt is the most personally damaging belief we can hold.

Monkey Conditioning: Behaviorism

Regaining our inherent self-confidence, self-belief, self-respect, and self-power is relatively easy, if we're willing to make the proper choices. The difficulty is in those decisions. Humans can behave very much like conditioned animals. It's for this reason that classical behaviorism gained such popularity. This school of thought essentially argues that the human condition is entirely a product of nature and nurture, and that people are conditioned to believe, behave, and otherwise execute life. There's no such thing as a higher principle or a need for self-actualization, because the human is but a shabby animal that possesses higher cerebral processing mechanisms than other creatures. We behave in habitual patterns, and treatment consists chiefly of changing the patterns.

The assertion seems simple: change behavior and you change the person. This has some very pragmatic applications, and we'll use it as we progress with the material at hand. However, just so there's no ambiguity, know that the underlying hypothesis, which asserts no higher principle, is as false a notion as any we'll ever encounter! On a similar note, now that we've reviewed a brief history of hypnosis, we're ready to move on and address common misunderstandings.

CHAPTER FOUR

Myths and Misconceptions

"Myths are a waste of time. They prevent progress."

— Barbra Streisand

I'd like to suggest that all hypnosis is fundamentally self-hypnosis. This idea isn't original to me, for one of the real pioneers of modern hypnosis, Dr. Milton Erickson, made this statement many years ago. The fact is that hypnosis is based on suggestibility, and you must be willing to accept the suggestions, or there will be no so-called trance state. That's not to say that gifted hypnotists aren't able to disarm any defenses you might have, but the fact remains that *you* are the key to a successful hypnotic session. However, there are still a number of myths and misconceptions that are worth covering.

Myth: I Can't Be Hypnotized

There are some who believe they can't be hypnotized, but this is incorrect. Everyone—or nearly everyone—can be. Hypnosis does require the ability to concentrate, so the only people who aren't susceptible are the very young or those who are of well below average intelligence and have problems focusing.

Myth: I Will Lose Control

One of the most commonly held myths is the idea that a person will do things under hypnosis that he wouldn't otherwise do. Anyone who has seen or heard about a stage hypnosis show will tell you that there were people barking like dogs and doing other things they wouldn't normally do. The fact is, they might not ordinarily behave in this manner, but they would if they could hide behind some excuse.

Let me provide an example: There are people who would really like to be funny, to be entertainers, to be the center of attention, but who are afraid of rejection. What if they fail? What if they aren't funny? What if they have stage fright? You get the picture. This personality type provides the perfect subject for the stage hypnotist. For while these folks hide behind the safety net of the hypnotist that "makes" them do things, they're able to perform in ways that they've always wanted to. Think about it this way: If the person volunteers to be a participant, isn't he or she already predisposed to play the role?

Stage hypnotists are skillful at selecting their subjects among the volunteers. Further, they're masters at detecting those subtle clues that predict the cooperation level of the volunteer. The truth is, you don't need hypnosis to achieve the same behavior that you can observe on the stage. In fact, the best of the entertainers have dumped the word *hypnosis* in favor of other terms, such as *suggestibility,* that better define their activities. However, the entire notion that someone else has control over you has no place in a self-hypnosis session, for you're both the hypnotist and the subject.

Myth: Only the Weak-Minded Can Experience Hypnosis

Some believe that hypnosis is something only weak-minded people experience. In fact, quite the opposite is true. Hypnosis is a natural state that's dictated by brain-wave activity, which I'll cover in greater depth in the next chapter. For now, this is what you need to know:

1. Normal consciousness is referred to in terms of brain-wave cycles as *beta.* This is a state equal to 15 cycles per second and up, typically 15 to 30 cycles per second.
2. Below beta is *alpha,* a state typically thought of as represented by 8 to 14 cycles per second of brain-wave activity when measured by an EEG.
3. Below alpha is *theta,* which is 4 to 7 cycles.
4. Below that is *delta.*

Alpha and theta brain-wave patterns are those manifest when the subject is in hypnosis. These brain-wave cycles are also those present when sleeping, and perhaps this partially explains why so many hypnotists use the word *sleep.* Entering hypnosis is indeed similar in the sense that brain-wave activity follows the same pattern, and visualization while in hypnosis can be very much like the rapid eye movement (REM) experience during sleep.

Myth: Hypnosis Is Just Deep Sleep

Over the years, I've used hypnosis in a variety of applications, including forensic work. I've hypnotized subjects who were able, in that condition, to provide significant additional factual material relevant to criminal investigations. Many of these subjects later told me that they didn't feel hypnotized. This shows the falsehood of the myth that hypnosis is a deep sleep. Indeed, you'll find that should you need to open your eyes for some reason, you'll do so and your mind will be clearer than if you'd been in the so-called normal state of consciousness, to say nothing of a deep sleep. In that sense, you're more prepared to respond appropriately to your environment.

You Are Always in Control!

Although we've now dispelled the most common myths about hypnosis, you should also know right from the start that you're always in control—you can always end a hypnosis session whenever you choose. Whether it's a guided session by me on the audio download that accompanies this book or an experience led by anyone else, including yourself, you can simply open your eyes and will the hypnosis session to be over.

CHAPTER FIVE

The Mechanics of Hypnosis

"The human mind is a channel through which things-to-be are coming into the realm of things-that-are."

— Henry Ford

Although it's an altered state of consciousness, hypnosis is, in fact, a natural state that can be objectively observed in brain-wave activity. Known as alpha and theta, this is not only a powerful state for mind training, deep relaxation, and accelerated learning opportunities, it's also a state that most of us move through several times each day. Before continuing, however, it's important to understand the different states of consciousness and how they relate to specific functions.

Altered States Of Consciousness

For some, an altered state of consciousness is a taboo. It signifies messing with the mind—and the mind is not to be messed with. I've always found such assertions naïve for the reason that every human being experiences various states of consciousness daily. When the typical person turns on the television, an altered state generally ensues. Indeed, children become conditioned to enter this state within minutes of beginning to watch TV.

Studies have demonstrated that even when children are hooked up to brain-wave monitoring devices such as EEG feedback and given substantial reward motivation to remain fully alert, in less than five minutes they'll fail to maintain ordinary wakefulness. The child will slip into what's commonly termed alpha consciousness (more on this in a moment).[1] When a person daydreams, falls into a light sleep or state of reverie, slowly wakes from a deep sleep, or fixates on almost anything, they're also usually in an altered state of consciousness.

So what is an altered state of consciousness? Typically, consciousness is divided into the four categories outlined in Chapter 4. Normal consciousness is beta, lightly modified consciousness is alpha, deep sleep is theta, and comatose states are delta. These levels are thought of in terms of brain-wave rates (cycles per second). To review: beta consciousness is normally 15 to 30 cycles per second, alpha is 8 to 14 cycles per second, theta is 4 to 8 cycles per second, and delta is less than 4. Now let's translate this schema into something meaningful outside the realm of definition.

Beta

In normal, ordinary wakeful states of consciousness, the mind operates from its most critical platform. It constantly judges input from self (inner talk) and others. It evaluates and reacts—indeed, it chiefly reacts. For even when we believe we're evaluating, more often than not, the assessment is settled before we begin. The belief system of the unconscious not only places a lens through which all matters will be judged, but it also hides behind a protective veil the information that may lead to mistaken decisions. That is, the unconscious mind during normal wakeful states is operating as a software program feeding the flow of everyday life through a mosaic of interpretations that are written chiefly upon avoidance and attraction principles (experienced and imagined). Therefore, when the conscious mind thinks something such as, *I can do this,* or *I'm good enough to excel and succeed,* the unconscious (or subconscious, if you prefer) sends an inner-talk message such as, *Really, good enough for what? How about . . . ? Do you remember . . . ?* and so on.

Maybe the unconscious sends that message due to some fear from the past or an imagined threat. Perhaps the harmful feedback is due to negative input from peers or parents. It's also possible that there's some deep sense of unworthiness stemming from a need to punish ourselves. It could be the result of a deep belief that conflicts with our desires, such as the longing to become successful and an inner line of logic that goes something like this: *If I want to be saved in heaven, I must sacrifice here and now. Further, the love of money is the source of all evil.* There could also be a myriad of other reasons and a virtual labyrinth of entanglement between them all. The fact is that in ordinary beta consciousness, very little new information can really get in.

Very little in these examples applies to alpha consciousness. In fact, just as an aside before going further, the methods of Superlearning and

Suggestopedia[2] clearly demonstrate the advantage of learning schoolroom information such as language, math, science, and the like in alpha consciousness states.

Alpha

Alpha consciousness is the state most refer to as the primary one experienced in hypnosis. Although hypnosis has been viewed from many perspectives and historically has held more than one definition, today it's agreed that it is a heightened state of suggestibility. This is just what it sounds like: in alpha consciousness, we're particularly prone to the acceptance of skillful suggestion. The nature of the experience depends on who's doing the suggesting. A hypnotherapist will offer healthy and positive ideas, while a salesperson trained in the art of hypnotic selling may put forth personally self-serving proposals.[3] The power of suggestion and the psychology of compliance are used every day in mass-marketing strategies to sell everything from illness to religion.[4]

When we're in an alpha state, whether naturally or artificially induced, our inner talk tends to slow down and become image oriented or guided as opposed to constantly self-initiated, albeit often unconsciously. And in modern society, we're exposed to a variety of stimuli that our ancestors never knew.

Much of today's television, radio, and print-media programming dwells on violence, sex, and so-called taboo issues. The word is *sensationalism*.

The more sensational the material, the better the reviews will be; the more money involved, the larger the audience will be, and so on. Rather systematically over the past 20 to 30 years, our threshold of arousal has risen due to systematic desensitization, forcing an ever-increasing thrust into areas of an explicit nature in order to maintain the sensational. Consequently, our inner talk, our fantasies, our very ideation has been influenced. This new tolerance for vengeance, anger, fear, violence, and sexuality has tilted our society. Values have been affected; and for many, the world is for living and taking while minimizing pain and maximizing pleasure. Twelve-year-old children walk into schools and gun down their teachers and schoolmates. Drugs, child prostitution, gang violence, and drive-by shootings are the chief worries of parents today. How did our society degenerate to this point?

Many psychologists, psychiatrists, sociologists, anthropologists, and for that matter, political scientists, have made vociferous outcries asserting the neurotic nature of our times. They're lining up in an attempt to end the media management of arousal thresholds and value orientation.

Television has probably the single largest impact on people today. It guides our purchases; provides most of the information we have about the world and any single issue or event; and merchandises everything from apparel to hairstyles, fashion to the common cold. It's normal to hear: "It's flu season, and it's coming to your town! Everyone will get it! You can relax and baby yourself, pamper your whims, take some needed time off, and maybe even cement your relationships, if you have XYZ on hand."

How much sickness do you think is sold in the same way that attitudes and beliefs are propagated through our media?

You may want to say, "Taylor, you're nuts. Television doesn't make anyone sick. You don't get the flu from a TV!" Fair enough. Let's look a little deeper. When a person is in a state of alpha, such as hypnosis, the science and literature show us clearly and without doubt that the body can be suggested to health or illness. A hypnotist can suggest a burn, then place an ice cube on the subject's arm, and a blister will appear.

As a practicing hypnotist, I personally witnessed phenomena that illustrate the mind's control over the body to the degree that suggesting a simple runny nose is, as Sherlock Holmes would say, "Elementary!" But in order to tie this suggestibility of alpha states in to the problems posed by television viewing, we should also take a look at another area of scientific inquiry that may surprise you.

As I stated earlier, studies have shown that the average individual will enter alpha brain-wave states within four minutes or less of being engaged by television.[5] If you think about it, this shouldn't come as a surprise. How many times has each of us seen someone—or been someone—who was so engrossed by the television that yelling was required to get their attention?

Getting back to alpha consciousness and cold season: I ask you again, how much illness do you think is sold in order to create a market for the medications?

It should be obvious that the state of alpha consciousness is not only natural but can be a beneficial time to put positive information into our bio-computing mind/brain. How we use this opportunity can be a matter of choice or habituation. I once saw a sign in the supermarket selling the publication *TV Guide*. The sign underneath the current issue said, "Check Out." A picture of a television with the initials *TV* within it was all that accompanied the sign. How many times have you heard or used the phrase, "I'll watch television and check out"? Check out, vacuum the mind—these are the sayings we all naturally associate with TV. Turn our minds over, let go of our concerns, and let someone else program them. Why check out? In alpha states of consciousness, endorphin levels increase. These hormones are the body's natural opiate system. They feel good—perhaps too good sometimes. Some have therefore argued that television is addictive.

Before we continue, let me provide a visual analogy that may be helpful. If you think of brain-wave activity as the number of lines on an inch of graph paper, then you have a visual image of mental activity, at least as we measure it with electroencephalographic instrumentation. Instead of thinking of the lines on paper, think in terms of a fence. The closer the lines are to each other, the smaller the holes in the fencing material. The more closely woven the fence, the more restrictive it is to both incoming and outgoing materials—in our analogy, let's say birds. The mind is very much like this. The tighter the wire enclosure, the less information (stimuli) we can process and remember. This is why super-learning states use alpha consciousness. As the brain-wave activity slows down, the holes in our fencing material become large and more information can get in.

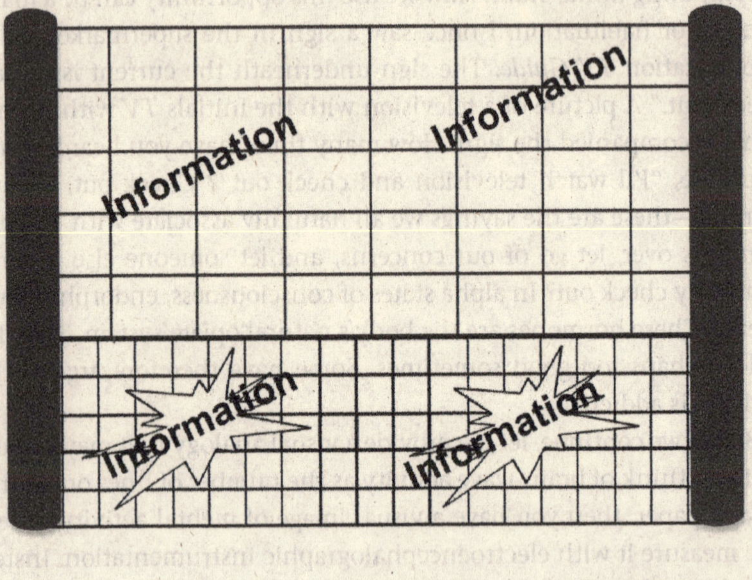

Theta

Theta consciousness is often associated with deep sleep and very deep levels of hypnosis or meditation. It's generally believed that the so-called superhuman feats of many spiritual masters, such as those reported eating hot coals and controlling bodily functions, are achieved while in theta consciousness. Indeed, mystics tend to teach that as the brain-wave patterns slow, the vibration of the body alters. By allegedly changing our physical vibration, many things thought to be impossible become possible. This is analogous to light vibrating at a rate much faster than glass; therefore, it passes through the glass. A stone, however, vibrates much slower than glass, consequently preventing it from passing through without breaking the glass. Thus, there's an arguable inverse proportion to brain-wave activity and body vibration. As the brain waves slow, the physical vibration rate is said to increase.

Delta

Delta consciousness is ordinarily thought of as comatose. For years, this state was believed to be so turned in on itself that outside stimuli went totally unnoticed, perhaps even unrecognized at any level. However, the work of Oliver Sacks showed the world that even in this state of consciousness, there is awareness. In his work, he used massive doses of dopamine and awakened (at least for a short time) most of his patients. Stranger than fiction, these individuals reported their various records and sensitivities to the history of their treatment, the hospital protocol, and their environment.[6]

Little is really known or understood about deep delta states of consciousness. However, clearly they're not dead or completely lacking awareness.

Techniques to Enter an Altered State

Self-hypnosis is all about learning how to enter the alpha brain-wave state and how to use it to create the desired experience. In the following chapter, I'll show you the basic techniques and some variations. As you practice, you'll soon learn the ones that you prefer; and with enough practice, you'll learn how to create your own methods. However, one of the most commonly used ways to slow down brain-wave activity from beta to alpha involves the use of visualization, so it's worth looking at this in a little more depth first.

Visualization

Visualization is the process of using the mind's eye to create images, scenes, emotions, and sensations. In his wonderful book *Psycho-Cybernetics,* Maxwell Maltz informs us that the mind can't distinguish an imagined experience, if imagined in sufficient detail, from reality.[7] In other words, the mind's memory stores the two as equally valid. Some of the work in neuro-method modeling has shown that imagined experiences can be so real as to produce muscular response. Using this technology, many athletes visualize their performance, see it vividly in the mind's eye, feel the tiny muscle groups respond to the mental experience, and in this way memorize the action. Indeed, some work has demonstrated a real physical advantage to imagining exercise. By doing so with vivid detail, a mental muscle workout begins to tone the body.

We've all experienced dreams that were so real that we thought twice about whether they occurred or not. Dreams of this nature are vivid, sensed in every way, and emotionally strong. Innate to our human makeup is this mental wiring that has the ability to generate synthetic experiences with the full power of actual experiences. Our memory records the event, imagined or real, and in this way the information becomes organized as part of our total experience.

Memory

Memory is a powerful force. Here, the important point is to recognize that it plays an essential role in our self-image, our expectations, our fantasies, and our general well being. Memory connections inform us of the continuity of being. Without this continuity, existence is episodic and could well be viewed as artificial. It's memory that reminds us of who we are, what's expected from us, how we've chosen to see the world, what our beliefs are, where we live, yesterday, the day before, and so on. Subtract memory, wake up with no recall, and each day becomes entirely different. Think about this for a moment.

When a person in deep hypnosis is given amnesia for certain events, the character of that individual changes. When artificial events are introduced, the character is again modified. Remember, when a deep trance subject is informed that he's being burned by the touch of an ice cube, a blister arises. When some multiple personality disordered patients switch personalities, their blood-sugar levels, eye color, and other physical attributes may change. Memory dictates the continuity that makes up our lives!

We never remember only factual information. The mind isn't a blank slate on which all actual events are recorded perfectly. Indeed, each time a memory is recalled, it's also changed. Hard evidence shows that recollection is also skewed by expectation, fear, anxiety, desire, and more. In a very real sense, we rehearse the memories we wish to, then remember them. Sometimes this rehearsal occurs prior to an event, sometimes it's at the time of the event, and sometimes it follows. Moreover, it's *always* adjusted with each recall and in line with the investment we put in each memory. In other words, memories thought to be very important have greater investments of energy, which is usually emotional.

Emotion

Emotion is a key component of memory. Even feelings not thought to be attached to the past event assert their influence. For example, some memories are pushed down deep in the mind, so deep that we don't consciously remember them, and this can be due to both the emotional tone of the event at the time and the time following the experience. Trauma victims often remember incidents—until they forget them. That may sound rather idiotic, but the fact is that we *must* remember in order to forget. Some level of operation within the mind defends our well-being by suppressing the memory. Then it remembers to keep the recollection suppressed and therefore develops a tactical structure to defend the forgotten incident.

Memory Suppression

Memories aren't erased—they are suppressed by a tactical operation. Built into this tactic are strategies to fend off inquiries. Often these strategies are self-defeating. The subliminal mind holds these unconscious beliefs, hidden memories, and tactical strategies to ostensibly protect our self-image and well-being. Sometimes the strategies are resistance oriented and sometimes they're attraction oriented, but they're always essentially diversions. From compensatory behavior to self-mutilation, they're *always* diversions!

A diversion is designed to stop us from closely examining the motives that underlie all action. Some of our motives are wired in survival-oriented objectives, while some are the result of deep mind links that through association camouflage or hide further, ulterior motives. We may also be driven by higher cortical intentions—like that of self-actualization.

Imagery in Hypnosis

Related to all this is the use of imagery, which has two essential roles in our context. The first is to provide a tool for generating memories of choice—feelings of well-being, for example. The second is to get in touch with aspects of ourselves that we may otherwise be unable to reach. When we visualize information, the image draws across all links for sensory input. Because of this, when we recall an event and allow ourselves to fully picture, feel, and otherwise sense it, the event will often bypass the critical mind and its defense mechanisms. Whole images may pop in and startle us, but linguistic approaches can only hope for bit-by-bit revelations such as those known as Freudian slips. And even then, we'll usually deny any connection between the slip (association) and more significant meaning.

One of the great healing powers of hypnosis is in its uncovering ability—largely, the ability to recover information as pictorial events unfold as on a movie screen, while detaching the individual from the emotion of the time. Hypnotic regressions and recall are therefore powerful tools in the healing arts.

Learning Visualization

As I've already stated, visualizing is a key component of self-hypnosis. It's used both in the induction stage and as a method to access inner life, as well as rewrite some memory information. Don't be concerned if you believe that you're not capable of visualizing. It's surprising how many people believe they don't see images when they close their eyes. It's also surprising the number who don't believe they dream. We all dream and must do so or lose our sanity. Remembering dreams, however, is quite different. There's no law of human nature that says we must remember our dreams.

Visualization is actually an easy skill to learn, and following are two exercises I strongly recommend.

Exercise: Visualization Training 1

Take a picture of some scene, say an outdoor vignette such as cooking over a fire. This must be from personal experience, so perhaps you'll choose a photograph from your last camping trip. In your imagination, enter the scene. Take the elements of the picture and imagine them all coming alive. Remember how you felt at that time, and bring those memories into your imagination. It's helpful if the associations are pleasant, so you really want to use a picture of an enjoyable event. So, stare at the scene until you feel it. If it was cold when you cooked over a fire outdoors, feel the chill. Let yourself shiver a little. Feel the warmth of the flames on your face. Once this is accomplished, close your eyes and hold the scene in the inner eye. If at first you don't succeed, try again. Repeat the process until you have the inner image fully on the screen of your mind.

Exercise: Visualization Training 2

The second approach is to take something you already have strong associations for that aren't emotional, but rather tactile in nature. Take, for example, a lemon. Hold the fruit in your hand and concentrate on it. Focus on how it feels. Think of how it tastes. Let the juices of the lemon shape your mouth. Smell it at close range. Look at its bright color; think of the sun and its color similarity. Allow yourself to associate any other information that comes with the lemon. Then close your eyes and see the lemon still in your hand, right in front of your face. Do this two or three times, and you'll begin to open the field of inner sight necessary for visualization.

Visualization for Self-Improvement

Assume we can now visualize. What do we picture? How often? When? Visualization should be a part of every day. By seeing a successful, rewarding day upon awakening, we're more likely to have one. Many people visualize misery in their lives without recognizing it. You might have some of these habits without realizing it. Do you dwell on fear thoughts, rehearse violent reprisals and revenge, take to bed angry actions from television and entertainment, or imagine the worst monsters entering your world? All of these actions are visualizations. What's more, when you imagine (visualize) fighting, the world brings you a fight. Somehow the conflict is never quite as you thought it would be, and once you learn this, it behooves you to imagine more peaceful events.

When we rehearse what we intend to say to someone, we're employing visualization. Using these skills to defend ourselves implies a need for protection. Well, the old universe is accommodating—here comes our chance to defend! When we use these skills to enhance our sense of belonging, participation in the glory of life, joy, and well-being, the universe somehow brings exactly that opportunity. We can call this the law of attraction. The fact is that through whatever mechanism, we often attract what we invest in through our imagery and/or push it away as a matter of resistance. Resistance can occur as a part of defense strategies or simply because deep down we do not believe we are deserving. Understanding this, it's clear that using visualization skills daily is something most of us already do. Consciously employing these tools for a directed purpose is what self-hypnosis is all about. All we're going to do is invest the energy differently.

CHAPTER SIX

Hypnosis 101 and Beyond

"The Game of Life is the game of boomerangs. Man's thoughts, deeds and words return to him sooner or later, with astounding accuracy."

— Florence Scovel Shinn

Now it's time to begin to learn the process of self-hypnosis, but first you should understand that the exercises in this program are voluntary. You must choose whether to do them or not. The success of this program doesn't depend upon me; it depends upon *you.* You'll choose whether to accept the suggestion and go deeper or experience phenomena—it will always be you who gets the pass or fail mark. That's important to remember, for you're not only in control, you're "doing the doing" that leads you deeper into these magical states of consciousness. And it is only by doing so that you will experience profound inner realms of safety and access more information than the ordinary mind can know. So altered states of consciousness associated with hypnosis are up to you. The brighter you are, the more you can concentrate. The more you're able to focus, the more creative and innovative a person you are, and the greater your success will be.

As a special bonus, I've created two special InnerTalk subliminal programs to assist you in learning self-hypnosis. We'll cover subliminal technology and InnerTalk in particular in Chapters 8 and 9, but all you need to know for now is that it's perfect for assisting you in learning new behaviors and the thought patterns conducive to this. These audio programs contain affirmations that will assist you in both learning self-hypnosis and in advancing your skills in that area. The affirmations are also included under all the tracks on the accompanying audio download, so you're benefitting from them every time you play one of the audio exercises. To obtain your copies of these InnerTalk programs, please go to **www.eldontaylor.com/HypnosisAndSubliminal**, where you may download them for free. To read the affirmations, please see the Appendix.

To work with these bonus InnerTalk programs, just play them in the background; no special attention is required. However, you should *not* play these particular InnerTalk programs whenever conscious attention is appropriate, such as when running machinery or driving a car. These two programs contain messages about deepening altered states and aren't appropriate for use at any time when you should be focusing on something else. (This isn't the case for the vast majority of the InnerTalk programs.)

These tracks contain the same set of affirmations, but one is set to music for daytime use and the other is set to the sounds of the ocean for nighttime use. (Of course, you can play the music during the night, if you wish, and the nature during the day—it's totally up to you. Most people, though, prefer to sleep to the nature track as the sound of the ocean isn't as distracting as the sound of music.) If possible, play one of these programs all night long while you sleep. You should also play one when you begin your own self-guided sessions.

Beginning Self-Hypnosis

Now that we've covered the power of the mind and the history/theory of hypnosis, it's time to learn the actual techniques. For our purposes here, hypnosis can be divided into five stages: pre-relaxation, induction, deepening, utilizing, and coming back. We'll cover each of these individually, and you'll see that the self-hypnosis session really does require all of them. However, as you continue to practice, you may find that you don't need to go through some of the stages in quite as much detail. In fact, you may find that eventually you can skim over the pre-relaxation and induction phases and reduce the deepening phase significantly. This will be in part due to the post-hypnotic cues, which we'll cover shortly, and also because with practice you'll find it easier to allow the process to happen. You will therefore need to set aside at least 30 minutes when you start using these techniques by yourself. In time, you'll be able to reduce this to about 10 minutes.

As you become more proficient, you will see for yourself that self-hypnosis really is a tool you can use almost anytime and anywhere. There are, of course, some obvious times it should *not* be used, such as when driving or operating machinery, but this is really just common sense.

Pre-Relaxation

Before beginning hypnosis, you should be focused on the fact that this is something you're choosing to do. You should also make a conscious intention at this time to simply allow the process to occur, as opposed to going in with the goal of forcing a particular result. Select a location where you'll be undisturbed and comfortable—maybe in a recliner chair or on your bed. If the room is a little cool, then get yourself a blanket. If you choose, you may also play some gentle music, burn some incense, and light some candles. While this is totally unnecessary for the hypnosis process itself, it's okay if this assists you in relaxing. You may even wish to supercharge the self-hypnosis process by playing a complementary subliminal program, either one you've created yourself or an InnerTalk program. (I'll cover this all in Part III of this book.)

When you're in a comfortable position, take a few slow breaths and close your eyes. Breathing is an important element for relaxing and meditation, so focus on taking slow, even breaths. Inhaling is all you need to help you relax and vitalize your body, while exhaling releases all the tension. I also like to think of breathing as being circular—breathing in, the energy is moving up my spine; breathing out, it's going forward and down my front.

Once you've started the relaxation process and are perfectly comfortable, you're ready to start inducing self-hypnosis.

Inducing Hypnosis

As I explained earlier, hypnosis is basically a process whereby you intentionally slow down brain-wave activity from beta to alpha. Once in this state, you're able to access information from your subconscious and replace information if you so choose. But how do you consciously slow down brain-wave activity?

Most people have observed the process of hypnosis, or at least how it's depicted in the movies. Oftentimes there will be some repetitive action—perhaps a flashing light, a swinging pendulum, or a spinning disc—and always the hypnotist is speaking in a slower-than-normal, calm voice. All of these techniques are designed to set the desired pace and encourage the brain-wave activity to slow down, so the pendulum swings slowly, the light flashes slowly, the disc spins slowly, and the voice speaks slowly! While the first three methods are great for eliminating the background distractions and assisting the individual in focusing on the hypnotic process, they aren't compulsory, and in fact aren't required at all during self-hypnosis. (However, if you'd like to experience this form of hypnotic induction, please visit **www.innertalk.com/self_hypnosis.html**.)

The technique I've found to be the most successful for slowing down brain-wave activity and entering a light hypnotic state is called "progressive relaxation." This doesn't require any special equipment and can be done anywhere at anytime. As I said, this technique is perfect for inducing hypnosis, but it's also great for calming yourself down when you find yourself in situations of high stress.

Rather than describing progressive relaxation to you, why don't we just try it so that you can experience this for yourself. I've included the full script for this session so that you can practice it for yourself later, but first I want you just to experience it.

Induction 1

The following exercise can be found on Track 1 of the accompanying audio download. You should note that while all the exercises recorded there are in the second person, when you do these exercises for yourself, you'll want to convert them to the first person. Therefore, "You become more and more relaxed," will change to: "I become more and more relaxed." The recordings are provided so that you may experience my techniques. They're recorded in the second person because—by the very nature of the audio recordings—the tracks aren't you speaking to yourself, but me teaching you. The idea is simply to experience it and learn how to induce yourself.

Now, put down the book and go to Track 1 on the audio download.

Please note: The exercises in this book that are marked with ≙ have been recorded on the accompanying audio download.

Now that you've experienced it for yourself, here is the script.

Exercise: Progressive Relaxation ≙

Instructions: You'll need to close your eyes, sit back or lie in a comfortable position, and remain undisturbed for at least 20 minutes. Get comfortable, and be prepared to enter a state of mind that's more profoundly relaxing than anything you have ever experienced. There's nothing more to do but repeat this script to yourself. Just internalize the concept—don't worry about memorizing it word for word. For now, the overlying story line is all that matters.

I just think, Relax. I feel the word as I think it into my body. Relax. There is nothing to do but relax. Allow the muscles in my body to just go limp; think, Relax. Now let's start at the top of my head and work throughout my body to produce a profound state of deep relaxation. I imagine that a bright, white column of light is descending from above and bathing the top of my head. It's warm and peaceful, the radiant sunlight. Everything is okay. It feels like a special soothing form of sunlight wrapping itself around me, beginning at the top of my head. As it touches me, envelops me, it moves down around the outer part of my body, and I can feel the warmth as I let go and allow the peacefulness of the moment to eliminate any thoughts that may be distracting.

Now the light begins to enter my body beginning at the top of my head. I close my eyes. My scalp completely relaxes. Relaxed . . . relaxed . . . and as the light moves down to the area of my throat and jaw, I may feel the need to swallow, and that's okay. I go ahead and swallow. I feel the warmth of the rays as they penetrate deep into every fiber of my being. I open my mouth slightly now, and think a little extra relaxation to my jaws and throat muscles. Just thinking Relax will aid me in letting everything go. Just allow the quietness of spirit to hold the moment. Relax, relax, relax. Now I just allow the special bathing light to move down into my neck and shoulders. My neck and shoulders go limp now, loose and limp. All tension, all concern disappears. The light just somehow seems to dissipate all negative energy and wash away any worry or concern.

For a moment, peace, balance, and harmony are mine. I am safe; I am secure. I think back to my scalp for a moment. I am already able to feel how much more relaxed my scalp and facial muscles are as a result of just a few moments in this relaxation session. My eyelids are heavy. My muscles are loose and limp. And I let go all over. I think of my eyelids—they are just too heavy to lift. There is nothing for me to do now but relax. I am learning to focus my thoughts. I am learning to train my body to respond to my thoughts. I am using my mental energy for more important things now than lifting my eyelids. Nevertheless, should I need to open them for any reason, I simply reallocate the use of energy.

So I'm safe and comfortable, but still quite aware of my surroundings. And this is ever more peaceful and ever more pleasant. Relax, relax. I let the light move down to my chest and lungs now, let it fill my being with peace and health. I just allow it to saturate every muscle, nerve, and fiber of my being; and I recognize it as it happens. I symbolically acknowledge this wonderful state of letting go even more, and thereby go deeper and deeper. Deeper and deeper I go into the innermost sanctuary of my being. And it feels so good. I breathe deeply for a moment. I feel my breath fill my lungs and hold that breath to the mental count of three.

I let it go slowly, counting from one to three mentally. Here I go. Breathe in . . . one . . . two . . . three . . . hold . . . one . . . two . . . three . . . exhale . . . one . . . two . . . three . . . hold . . . one . . . two . . . three. . . . While doing this three more times, I find myself going into an even deeper and more peaceful state, a place of mind so tranquil that I will want to return here often. This is a state of being so peaceful that I will find a few moments here will entirely refresh and invigorate me. I will even feel like this brief session renewed me as much as a long nap.

Okay, I let the light work its way down to the tip of my toes, the very tips of my toes. I feel it moving down, and I can now guide it the rest of the way. I guide it right out to the very tip of each toe. As I do this, I continue deepening my relaxation. My unconscious mind knows exactly what to do.

The conscious mind knows what the subconscious allows it to know. My deepest memories, all I have ever learned and much more, are stored away in that vast reservoir of knowledge and wisdom known as the unconscious or subconscious mind. From here on out, my conscious mind can continue to work the light all the way down and right on out through the tips of my toes. I continue to breathe slowly and deeply; and as the light fully fills all of my being, I acknowledge the success my conscious mind has achieved. I let it rest with gratitude for the work it has done and all that it has achieved.

Each time I enter this state, I will find it easier and easier to go deeper and to do so faster and faster. In just a few sessions, I will find it natural to go deep, deep, deep down into my inner sanctuary. Almost as quickly as the snap of my fingers . . . deep, deep, deep into those special inner centers of knowing, of wisdom, of peace, balance and harmony. Each time I enter this state, I will learn more about myself and be able to more clearly find balance and achieve peace in everything I do and think. In fact, the power and peace that comes from being in this profound state of relaxation will accumulate, and soon I will be able to come here for many treasures that most only wish they could find.

I am now gaining the ability to use my own mind to its fullest potential. The thin wall between the conscious and subconscious is becoming thinner. And soon, every helpful possibility that both levels of awareness can bring to any situation will be mine. All of this simply amazes me. In my next session, I will find it easier and easier to go deep, deep, deep down into my personal place of peace, my personal inner sanctuary. Thus, the training from each session will also accumulate, and I will very quickly be able to master self-hypnosis. In fact, as a matter of self-cue in the next session, I will simply use the word relax, and everything that I am now feeling will automatically flow through my being. The word relax is my cue. In the next session, I will say, "Relax," and I will easily and peacefully close my eyes and just let go. I will go right to where I am now automatically, deep, deep down inside the absolute safety of my own personal, peaceful sanctuary.

But for now, it's time to come back. I will begin some self-conditioning by returning to the backward count from five to one. And upon one, my eyes will open, and I'll be fully back in the so-called normal state of consciousness. All right, number five beginning to return; number four coming back now; number three, and although it's very natural to want to remain here and even go deeper at this time, coming all the way back, all the way back. Number two, coming back now. Number one, eyes open, eyes open, wide awake, wide awake now, feeling very, very good in every way . . . very good in every way. I just sit here for a moment. Take a deep breath.

Induction 2

Here is another induction technique. Once again, I've included this on the accompanying audio download, and I suggest that you experience the induction first before reading about it. This is the kind of process that certain hypnotists will use on their clients, and it's really not something you'd use for self-hypnosis. However, as you'll see, this is a powerful way to discern those people who will make better hypnotic subjects. It's the kind of technique that a stage hypnotist would use.

So stop reading now, and go to Track 2 on the audio download.

Now that you've experienced it for yourself, here's the script. As this isn't an exercise you'd do on yourself, I've left it in the second person.

Exercise: Double-Bind Induction ≙

Instructions: Sit in a comfortable, upright position. Be sure your back is straight. This isn't a test; it's a demonstration. Therefore, it's critically important that you follow my instructions literally. You don't have to, but if you don't, you'll only cheat yourself. You will not be asked to close your eyes or anything like that. Think of it as a sort of Simon Says game. Be sure your hands are resting on your legs with the palm side up.

Look at your hands and concentrate on the palms and how they feel. I want you to make a decision. Which one, the left or the right, feels lighter than the other? One will be heavier on your leg and one will be relatively light. Choose the lighter one, and turn all your attention and focus onto it now. Stare at it for the moment; stare at it and marvel at how light it feels.

I want you to use the unlimited power of imagination now. I want you to imagine that there is a very powerful magnet in the palm of your hand. It is, in fact, a part of your hand. It's very powerful, so powerful that you can almost see the lines of magnetic force spreading outward from the center of your palm. And now, with just a little extra imagination, I want you to imagine another very strong magnet on your forehead, just above and directly between your eyes. Now imagine and feel the pull of these two magnets and make it real with the absolutely unlimited power of your mind. Feel it as it lifts and pulls your hand from your leg, slowly at first, but steadily lifting and pulling your hand toward your face, toward your head, right up to your forehead. Now make a decision: Is the magnetic force stronger from the hand to the head or from the head to the hand? Decide—decide now. Okay, you can stop. Lower your arm and hand.

Double-Bind Suggestibility Test

Induction 2 is an actual procedure and among my favorites. It can be set up so that once the hand touches the head, the eyes close and the person goes to a deep level of inner quiet and peace. It's a matter of simply making that suggestion. The point of this exercise, however, wasn't to show you an induction so much as a general technique. The mind can be funny in the sense that it can fool us. Think for a moment. Was the magnetic force stronger from the hand or the head? This is called a double bind, because it doesn't matter which you decide is strongest. The fact is that when you make the decision, you've acknowledged the presence of a magnetic force. You have given this force power, and it can appear that the operator—me, in this instance—has some control over your body. This is all a matter of a suggestion that you give power.

The double bind works well for precisely the reason that almost everyone will make a choice when given the chance. Think: you chose one of your hands, just as you decided which magnetic force was the strongest. Further, people will almost always choose between the options given.

You can feed into natural functions, and that, too, may provide the appearance of control over a subject's body. Take, for example, our last session, where I suggested that you might need to swallow and it was okay to do so. Well, of course you're going to need to swallow as you relax, and predictably so. Obviously, I didn't control your body, although it can sometimes seem as though that's the case.

Deepening Hypnosis

As you begin to learn self-hypnosis, you'll find it relatively easy to enter into a very light hypnotic state. However, in order to do any real work, you'll normally want to go deeper. There are several different techniques for this, and you'll probably want to experiment before you decide which one you prefer. If you aren't very confident in your visualization abilities, it's perfectly okay to simply count yourself down. Following is a simple script that you can use for this purpose. Given the simplicity of this exercise, it hasn't been recorded on the accompanying audio download. All you need to do is read it through until you're familiar with the process, then put the book down, close your eyes, and try it for yourself. Do *not* record this and then play it back, because the purpose of this book isn't just to learn about hypnosis, but to learn *self*-hypnosis.

Exercise: Countdown Deepening

As I count down from ten to one, I will go down deeper and deeper into hypnosis. Even when I think I cannot relax any more, as soon as I count down another number, I will find myself going deeper and deeper. So on the count of ten, I will go deeper and deeper, feeling so relaxed and calm, deeper and deeper. And now nine, I go down and down, feeling even more tension leaving my body . . . down and down, deeper and deeper. With every outward breath, I find myself becoming more and more relaxed. And number eight, being very aware that I have become even more relaxed, so comfortable, so protected, deeper and deeper. Number seven, sliding ever deeper into relaxation. I am no longer questioning my ability to become more and more relaxed, simply allowing the process to occur. Number six, breathing in and then breathing out, and going deeper, deeper, deeper. All is well. I am comfortable, more and more relaxed. Number five, now all the tension has gone, and yet I still move deeper and deeper into a more relaxed state. Allowing, accepting, perfectly content. Number four, once again becoming even more relaxed, moving deeper and deeper into a state of pure relaxation. Breathing slowly and comfortably. As I breathe out, I feel more and more relaxed. As I breathe in, I breathe in more and more relaxation. Number three, deeper and deeper into relaxation, feeling calm, secure, safe. Number two, ever so relaxed, yet perfectly aware. Soothing, gentle, relaxing, moving deeper and deeper. And number one, feeling more deeply relaxed than I ever thought possible.

The reason you might think you're unable to visualize really comes down to expectation. Using your inner eye is simply very different from normal sight. Once you stop expecting to see in the same way, you'll find your skills improving. In fact, as you practice using visualization in self-hypnosis, you may find this technique comes so easily that you'll wonder why you ever thought you weren't able to do it. So here's a deepening exercise that uses visualization. Once again, just read through the script until you're very familiar with the story line, then put this book aside, close your eyes, and try the technique for yourself.

Exercise: Visualization Deepening

I am perfectly relaxed, my eyes are closed, and my breathing is slow and even. I find myself at the top of a terraced garden. Stretching out in front of me is a vast area of the most beautiful flowers. There are ten stone steps running down the center of the garden, and I start toward them. The flowers smell divine, and the warm sun on my face is perfectly comfortable. Walking down the path, I come across the first step. As I step down, I feel myself becoming more relaxed and more comfortable. The warm sun takes me deeper into relaxation, as does the light breeze on my face. Feeling more and more relaxed, I continue down the garden steps.

I take the second step down, enjoying the feeling of being even more relaxed and at peace. I continue following the path, no cares in the world. As the path slopes downward, I find myself relaxing more and more. Soon I come to the third step, and as I step down, I am very aware of a great sense of peace and relaxation. Going down the path, I find myself going deeper and deeper into a state of relaxation and tranquility. I step down the fourth step and am amazed by how relaxed and calm I am. The fragrance is so sweet, and I am so very comfortable, so very content . . . perfectly relaxed . . . deeper and deeper into relaxation.

Down the fifth step, I am going deeper and deeper into relaxation, more and more calm, no tension at all. Perfectly relaxed and simply enjoying the beautiful garden. Down the sixth step, even the air is soft and gentle, easing me in a deeper and deeper state of relaxation. The colors of the flowers becoming even more vivid, filling my vision, the fragrance making me feel even more relaxed.

Going deeper and deeper, I go down the seventh step. I have never felt so relaxed, calm, and at peace. The tranquility of the garden and the tranquility of my inner being are becoming one. More and more relaxed. Going down the eighth step, even the stone path feels soft and cushionlike. All of this helps me to feel ever more relaxed. Deeper and deeper, more and more relaxed, peace fills my being.

Down the ninth step, the feeling of relaxation continues to grow, deeper and deeper. The air is so comfortable around me. Every time I breathe in, I inhale the gentle, relaxing fragrance. Feeling ever more relaxed, I take the tenth step. I am feeling more relaxed than I ever have, feeling more relaxed than I ever thought possible. I take a deep breath in, capturing this moment, so that in the future, whenever I wish, all I have to do is think of my garden and I will find myself back here in this amazingly relaxed state.

As you become more practiced at self-hypnosis, you will rely less and less on actual scripts. You will find yourself able to enter hypnosis more and more easily, and you will be able to design your own story lines, your own secret getaway, where you can go whenever you need some peace and tranquility. You'll also be able to come up with the place where you can go do your personal work, where you'll feel safe doing so. Maybe you'll create a spot where you can communicate with your higher self, access lost memories, or perhaps even communicate with your guides. It's up to you.

The vast majority of times, hypnosis (with a hypnotist or using self-hypnosis) is performed by going down deeper and deeper, but it doesn't have to be this way. One of the programs I offer at Progressive Awareness Research is called *Hyperemperia*. This is a guided-imagery program where I lead you up and up, expanding as opposed to contracting. Once consciousness is expanded, you're given time to go and speak to your guides and masters. I've heard from a number of customers how much they enjoyed this program, and some have even reported experiences where their guides communicated very meaningful information.

Using Post-Hypnotic Cues

In addition to relaxing or accessing information that you may have forgotten, hypnosis can also be used for post-hypnotic cues. You can put in a prompt to be used after the hypnosis session, perhaps to enhance your next hypnosis session, or maybe to assist you with something in your normal life. This technique can produce some significant and immediate results. Post-hypnotic cues can be placed in any part of the hypnosis process—induction, deepening, utilizing, or coming back.

If you look back at the script for the Progressive Relaxation exercise, you'll see that I use post-hypnotic cues twice. In these instances, they're there to enhance your next hypnosis experience.

Post-Hypnotic Cue 1

Each time I enter this state, I will find it easier and easier to go deeper, and to do so faster and faster. In just a few sessions, I will find it natural to go deep, deep, deep down into my inner sanctuary. Almost as quickly as the snap of my fingers. Deep, deep, deep into those special inner centers of knowing, of wisdom, of peace, balance and harmony. Each time I enter this state, I will learn more about myself and be able to more clearly find balance and achieve peace in everything I do and think. In fact, the power and peace that comes from being in this profound state of relaxation will accumulate, and soon I will be able to come here for many treasures that most only wish they could find.

Post-Hypnotic Cue 2

In my next session, I will find it easier and easier to go deep, deep, deep down into my personal place of peace, my personal inner sanctuary. Thus, the training from each session will also accumulate, and I will very quickly be able to master self-hypnosis. In fact, as a matter of self-cue in the next session, I will simply use the word <u>*relax,*</u> *and everything that I am now feeling will automatically flow through my being. The word* <u>*relax*</u> *is my cue. In the next session, I will say, "Relax," and I will easily and peacefully close my eyes and just let go.*

I also used a post-hypnotic cue in the Visualization Deepening exercise.

Post-Hypnotic Cue 3

I am feeling more relaxed than I ever have, feeling more relaxed than I ever thought possible. I take a deep breath in, capturing this moment, so that in the future, whenever I wish, all I have to do is think of my garden and I will find myself back here in this amazingly relaxed state.

There are, of course, a variety of reasons you may have decided to learn self-hypnosis. Maybe you have to give some kind of presentation, and you're terrified of public speaking. In this case, a good cue would be: "I remember this feeling of calm and relaxation, and whenever I bring my thumb and forefinger together, I will experience this feeling again. In fact, whenever I have to give a presentation, I will remember to bring my thumb and forefinger together; and as soon as I do, I will be calm and relaxed again and will remain this way throughout my presentation."

If you tend to lose your temper too easily, you could say, "Whenever I feel that I am going to lose my temper, when anyone says something that would normally have me losing my temper, I will simply tap my thigh gently, and I will automatically be calm and relaxed—as calm and relaxed as I am now. The feeling of anger will simply dissipate, and I will find a solution that is more gentle and in line with the person I wish to be."

If you tend to eat when you're under stress—perhaps you've always reached for a piece of cake or some other treat when you're upset—then maybe you could say, "When I am feeling stressed and think that eating something will help, I lick my lips gently, and I find myself feeling calm and relaxed, so calm and relaxed that all desire for the cake is gone, so calm and relaxed that I find I would prefer a glass of water. So all I have to do is lick my lips very gently, and I will find myself calm, relaxed, and perfectly in control."

As you can see, there are many ways that you can use post-hypnotic cues to enhance your daily life. You're restricted only by your own imagination.

Eliminating Distractions

Sometimes when you're trying to enter self-hypnosis, you can become very aware of background sounds—sounds that never bothered you before, but which you suddenly find very intrusive. Incorporating these noises into your induction or deepening stages can actually enhance the hypnotic effort. For example, let's say there's traffic outside, your office clock ticks a lot louder than you thought, and from time to time you can hear people in the room next to yours. Here's a suggested deepening script, using the simple countdown that will take all this into consideration:

Exercise: Deepening to Eliminate Distractions

Now, as I count down from ten to one, I will go down deeper and deeper into hypnosis. Even when I think I cannot be even more relaxed, as soon as I count down another number, I will find myself going deeper and deeper. Before I start counting down, I become aware of all the background noises that may disturb my session. I notice the ticking of the clock, and rather than disturbing me, each tick of the clock will assist me in going deeper and deeper into relaxation. I am aware of the traffic noise outside my window, and as I go deeper and deeper into hypnosis, this noise will become a gentle hum, pulling me into a more and more relaxed state. I am aware that sometimes I may hear the people next door, and this too will just assist me in going deeper into relaxation. Nothing will bother me. I am fully in charge. As long as I wish to go into hypnosis, into a state of peace and utter calm, then that is what I will do.

So on the count of ten, I will go deeper and deeper, feeling so relaxed and calm, deeper and deeper. And now nine, I go down and down, feeling even more tension leaving my body, down and down, deeper and deeper. With every outward breath, I find myself becoming more and more relaxed. And number eight, being very aware that I have become even more relaxed, so comfortable, so protected, deeper and deeper. Number seven, sliding ever deeper into relaxation, no longer questioning my ability to become more and more relaxed, simply allowing the process to occur. All of the background noises have now just slipped away, working to take me deeper and deeper into relaxation.

Number six, breathing in and then breathing out, and going deeper, deeper, deeper. All is well. I am comfortable, more and more relaxed. Number five, now all the tension has gone, and yet I still move deeper and deeper into that most relaxed of states. Allowing, accepting, perfectly content. Number four, once again becoming even more relaxed, moving deeper and deeper into a state of pure relaxation. Breathing slowly and comfortably. As I breathe out, I feel more and more relaxed. As I breathe in, I breathe in more and more relaxation. Number three, deeper and deeper into relaxation, feeling calm, secure, safe. Number two, ever so relaxed, yet perfectly aware. Soothing, gentle, relaxing, moving deeper and deeper. And number one, feeling more deeply relaxed than I ever thought possible.

So, as you can see, you can take any outside distraction and use it to enhance your hypnosis session. You don't have to wait to be in the perfect setting. This means that you can use these techniques while waiting for an airplane, before some major competitive event, or even while your spouse is playing with the children in the next room!

Utilizing Self-Hypnosis

Visualization techniques are often used to induce hypnosis in another individual as well as in self-hypnosis. They can also be used to deepen the hypnotic state, and the earlier Visualization Deepening exercise does precisely that. But now it's time to learn some practical applications for self-hypnosis. One very simple but effective use is to imprint your subconscious mind with an affirmation of a character trait you'd like to have, and the next exercise will teach you to do just this.

First, you must choose your affirmation. It's important, so write it down before beginning the exercise. Choose your words with care, and make them all positive. Make the affirmation itself as short as possible. For example, if you wish to have more confidence, you might use an affirmation like this: *I am confident.* When you use your affirmation, feel it. Sense what it is saying in every dimension. In other words, feel the confidence fill your being as the affirmation circulates throughout you.

This exercise is recorded on the accompanying audio download, so before you read the transcript for this session, please just experience it. Lie down or recline in a comfortable fashion, and loosen your clothing. You may choose to play soothing music or nature sounds in the background during this exercise. If available, try also burning pleasant incense. Dim or eliminate lighting. Start playing Track 3 on your audio download. Close your eyes and follow the procedure.

Now that you've experienced the session, here's the dialogue in the first person for your further use.

Exercise: Using Affirmations in Hypnosis ≙

Instructions: Read the procedure, then select a quiet place where you won't be disturbed for at least 20 minutes. Before you begin this exercise, set an alarm clock for 20 to 25 minutes. You'll use the clock to return you to normal consciousness until the time period becomes conditioned, which usually only takes three to four sessions. When the alarm sounds, open your eyes slowly. Let yourself just rest for about five minutes before getting back into the affairs of the day.

With my eyes closed, I imagine myself resting outdoors with a warm and balmy sun bathing my body. I can feel its warmth touching me all over. My breathing is gentle and even. My exhalations provide life-force energy for the plant world, just as my inhalations provide life-force energy for me. A certain synergy exists between me and the world around me, a sort of symbiotic relationship. I sense this and imagine feeling my being extending in and out of all life with every breath.

I breathe deeply and evenly for a moment . . . in to the count of five, hold to the count of five, exhale to the count of five. I smile slightly as I do this and repeat this three times.

Now, I sense a bright, luminescent, pure gold light coming down from above and entering at the top of my head. I feel the light enter and begin to move down through my body—into my neck, down the back, through my legs, and right on down to the tip of my toes. And with one more deep inhalation, the light energy expands outward, radiating several feet from my body. I sense my entire being is aglow.

I open my mouth slightly and swallow. I let the muscles in my scalp completely relax. I think, Relax—relax now, and they all relax. I continue the relaxation as though it were some magical potion that I had just swallowed. Relax the jaw muscles, the throat muscles, the neck, the shoulders, the arms, the back, the abdomen, the buttocks, the thighs, the calves of the legs, the ankles, the feet, and every single toe. To each area I simply send the thought: Relax—relax now.

With the entire body relaxed, there is nothing to do. Right now is the time to do nothing. Just let go and be. Relaxed. And with a tiny effort of mind, I now concentrate all of my being into one of my toes. I concentrate so wholly, totally in that toe that every minute sensation is sensed by my entire being. I do this with one toe on each foot and then place all of my consciousness in the area of my solar plexus.

From the solar plexus, the heart region is above. I alternate my consciousness between my solar plexus and my heart. From this perspective, I focus on my one, important affirmation [insert your affirmation] and begin to see it flow back and forth. I see it, and I hear it. As soon as I see and hear it distinctively, I allow it to begin the journey throughout my body. So—it disappears—but it is still there. It travels from cell to cell on a journey throughout the body. It will be back to travel again. In fact, throughout my session from this point on, my affirmation, [insert your affirmation], will travel over and over again through my body. As it approaches my consciousness, it may again become visual and audible. But that is of no matter; I have let it go. It goes to announce to all of my being—this is the way it is.

Now I just relax, allowing the affirmation to travel through my own body, imprinting the core of my being with this new belief.

Sometimes I am aware of it; other times I am not. All I am doing is enjoying this state of peace and calm. When the alarm goes off, it will not startle me. Rather, it will act as a gentle trigger to return me to normal consciousness. When the alarm announces, I will open my eyes slowly. I will then just rest for about five minutes before getting back into the affairs of the day.

But for now, I just relax and enjoy . . .

The best way to condition yourself with hypnotic suggestions is repetition. Try to do this affirmation exercise daily for a week or two. If you do, you'll find that occasional touch-up sessions can be undertaken almost anywhere and under almost any conditions. This can have many practical applications, to say nothing of the physical and mental benefits.

Self-Suggestion

Self-suggestion is the next extension of self-hypnosis, and for some, it's all that's needed. The power of this technique is in the repetition of a thought or phrase. This method is advocated in positive-thinking books. Take a phrase like our confidence affirmation, and repeat it over and over in your mind. Write it down, and carry it on a card. Make a list of benefits that accompany the accomplishment and carry that with you, too. Get out your periodicals and newspapers, and find pictures that represent your goal. Cut out these images, and write your affirmation under them. Place pictures with your affirmation on the refrigerator, on the bathroom mirror, in your automobile, and anywhere else that you'll regularly encounter them. Each time you repeat the affirmation or encounter it, your mind records the information. You begin to identify with the images—the pictures. In this way, the automatic servomechanism that you might call the machinery of the subconscious records and begins to script your inner talk and self-belief around your repeated affirmations.

Uncovering Information

Once you've learned to put yourself into hypnosis, you can make further use of this state. There are two exercises I believe to be very powerful self-empowerment techniques. The first is for purposes of uncovering or recovering hidden information, and I like to call this Power Imaging. We offer several Power Imaging titles on my website, but they're all for very specific goals. Here, you can use the process for any goal you wish. The second exercise creates, shall we say, a matrix for realizing some event like personal success. But first, let's look at Power Imaging.

Exercise: Power Imaging ≙

Instructions: This exercise is Track 4 on the accompanying audio download, and again, I suggest using it before reading and practicing the script that follows. This is best done after you've been through the induction and deepening techniques you have already learned. Once you've listened to the audio track, read the exercise, and then close your eyes and follow the practice as given. Use the technique you practiced in the preceding exercise, but rather than focusing on an affirmation, simply imagine yourself in a comfortable chair.

Behind me is a slide projector. It has a remote control, and I am holding this control. Before me is a screen. The slide projector holds thoughts, images, feelings, and pictures that are associated together. I do not remember all the slides. I do not know in advance how they are organized. I am simply going to watch this slide review. I am not even sure how many slides there are.

[Now take a thought, maybe an idea of what you'd like to become, such as wealthy or popular. Or you can take a fear, but if you do this, always remember that your remote control will shut off the projector any time you wish.]

I put the [ambition or fear] into the context of a picture in my mind. This is the first slide. The projector will automatically take this slide and associate all other relevant slides appropriate at this time and organize them in a meaningful way. Now I may not understand the scope, but I will just trust that it is significant.

I put the first slide up on the screen by simply seeing it there as I imagined it. I spend a moment getting fully involved with the image. I feel it, smell it, remember it fully. I can enrich this image as much as I would like. I can add cheering, feel goose bumps, and the like. I fully bring this first slide to life—on the screen of the mind. Once I have accomplished this, then I change the image by pushing the remote control. I can connect my thumb and forefinger to assist me with the imagery. Press the thumb slightly against the forefinger, and the slide changes. Close my hand tightly, and the projector shuts off.

It is okay to wonder what slide may come next, but I do not force anything. I simply allow the slides to come as they wish. I may be surprised. I always remember, though, that I am in control. If I ever find the slides too difficult to watch, I will simply close my hand tightly and shut the projector off. Once the projector is shut off, I will open my eyes slowly. I allow myself to rest there for about five minutes before getting back to the affairs of the day.

This exercise provides a window on our desires, ambitions, and fears. It may reveal self-limiting beliefs that we no longer wish to maintain. It may produce images that we wish to desensitize. Use the next exercise to do either.

Exercise: Personal Empowerment

Instructions: Follow the same instructions as with the Power Imaging exercise, but omitting the audio portion, since this exercise is not on the audio download.

I am in a sophisticated studio. I am about to review the footage taken of me at a special event. I will be able to edit this footage and make it into exactly what I wish.

The studio is fully equipped with the best audio and video production equipment. The screen is larger than any theater I have ever seen. The screen wraps around me, and when the footage begins, I will find that it is as if I am actually there. Unlike movie theaters, my studio is able to reproduce the events in such a way that it is almost impossible to detect the difference between the re-creation and the actual experience.

I am in a comfortable chair. I have a thought-controlled interface with all of the equipment. As such, as quickly as I wish something altered, edited, or changed; new footage added; or whatever I deem appropriate, I think about it and it is ready to replay just as I desire.

I have chosen my footage. There are virtually limitless programs to play or record my information.

I know that very special people have a studio just like the one I am visiting. Some are athletes, some are businesspeople, some are scientists, and some are artists. Whatever their profession, the best of them all have their own inner-mind studios. The reason is simple: they know they can create their work there first. By so doing, they minimize the confusion, the risk, and the obstacles that they might meet in the outer world. So an athlete comes here to generate the footage that represents his or her perfect play. A businessperson creates the movie of their success. Some people come here to review old dramas and change them. Sometimes they shift only their feelings, and sometimes they alter the scenes. For some, this is where old memories are desensitized by viewing the footage with different emotions—say, forgiveness instead of blame, guilt, and shame. Here is where they put the wisdom of the eternal into their understanding. Here is where they gain freedom from imprisoning feelings, fears, and thoughts.

So I now come here with an image derived from experience, one that has held me back—whether it is a fear or an early childhood memory that still grips me, this is where I will desensitize it. I do so by simply reviewing the image and editing the emotions until I have an end product that I feel good about. This is then stored in the memory banks and becomes the image that my mind begins to work with. Whatever I wish to achieve or experience, this is where I also create those scenes—just as I want them to be.

Now I begin to review the footage. Anything that does not please me, I change. I empower myself with sensory-rich detail. I hear the crowd applauding or feel true forgiveness, whatever is appropriate.

I play the footage back once I have edited it. I can edit it as many times as I like. I stay with it until it is perfect—just as I want it. Once I have done this, I let it go. I leave the studio and wait for another day to work on something else.

If my footage requires more than one visit to get it just the way I wish it had been, or just as I want it to be, then I can come back as often as necessary to accomplish this. However, I will not go on to other areas until I am satisfied with my work on each item of business in the order I bring it to the studio.

Coming Back from Hypnosis

When using self-hypnosis, it's best to have a definite end of some kind to the session. In the Progressive Relaxation exercise I gave earlier, I also brought you out of hypnosis:

Exercise: Exiting Hypnosis

Each time I enter this state, I will find it easier and easier to go deeper and to do so faster and faster. In just a few sessions, I will find it natural to go deep, deep, deep down into my inner sanctuary. Almost as quickly as the snap of my fingers . . . deep, deep, deep into those special inner centers of knowing, of wisdom, of peace, balance and harmony. Each time I enter this state, I will learn more about myself and be able to more clearly find balance and achieve peace in everything I do and think. In fact, the power and peace that comes from being in this profound state of relaxation will accumulate, and soon I will be able to come here for many treasures that most only wish they could find.

I am now gaining the ability to use my own mind in its fullest potential. The thin wall between the conscious and subconscious is becoming thinner. And soon, every helpful possibility that both levels of awareness can bring to any situation will be mine. All of this simply amazes me. In my next session, I will find it easier and easier to go deep, deep, deep down into my personal place of peace, my personal inner sanctuary. Thus, the training from each session will also accumulate, and I will very quickly be able to master self-hypnosis. In fact, as a matter of self-cue in the next session, I will simply use the word <u>*relax,*</u> *and everything that I am now feeling will automatically flow through my being. The word* <u>*relax*</u> *is my cue. In the next session, I will say, "Relax," and I will easily and peacefully close my eyes and just let go. I will go right to where I am now automatically, deep, deep down inside the absolute safety of my own personal, peaceful sanctuary.*

But for now, it's time to come back. I will begin some self-conditioning by returning to the backward count from five to one. And upon one, my eyes will open, and I'll be fully back in the so-called normal state of consciousness. All right, number five beginning to return; number four coming back now; number three, and although it's very natural to want to remain here and even go deeper at this time, coming all the way back, all the way back. Number two, coming back now. Number one, eyes open, eyes open, wide awake, wide awake now, feeling very, very good in every way . . . very good in every way. Just sit here for a moment. Take a deep breath.

As you'll remember, I also included some post-hypnotic cues. You can, of course, decide for yourself what cues you want to use. However, sometimes it may be appropriate not to bring yourself all the way out. Sometimes when I'm using self-hypnosis right before going to sleep, I'll use a post-hypnotic cue during the induction that allows this process to happen naturally.

The following script is a good way to extend the hypnosis session into your sleep. If your purpose was to uncover some information, then this will often allow the answers to come up in your dreams.

Exercise: Transitioning Hypnosis to Natural Sleep

Just think, Relax. Feel the word as I think it into my body. Relax. There is nothing to do but relax. Allow the muscles in my back to just go limp; think, Relax. Now I'll start at the top of my head and work throughout my body to produce a profound state of deep relaxation. If I fall asleep as I enter hypnosis, this is okay. My subconscious mind knows exactly what I wish to achieve in this session, and if I fall asleep, my subconscious will continue with the work. In this instance, the answers I am looking for will appear in my dreams, and they will be easy for me to understand.

But for now, I imagine that a bright white column of light is descending from above and bathing the top of my head. It's warm and peaceful, the radiant sunlight. Everything is okay. It feels like a special, soothing form of sunshine wrapping itself around me, beginning at the top of my head. As it touches me, envelops me, it moves down around the outer part of my body, and I can feel the warmth as I let go and allow the peacefulness of the moment to banish any thoughts that may be distracting.

Now the light begins to enter my body, beginning at the top of my head. I close my eyes. My scalp completely relaxes. Relaxed, relaxed, and as the light moves down to the area of my throat and jaw, I may feel the need to swallow, and that is okay. I go ahead and swallow. I feel the warmth of the rays as they penetrate deep into every fiber of my being. I open my mouth slightly now and think a little extra relaxation to my jaws and throat muscles. Just thinking <u>*Relax*</u> *will aid me in letting everything go. I allow the quietness of spirit to hold the moment. Relax, relax, relax. Okay now, I just allow the special bathing light to move down into my neck and shoulders. My neck and shoulders go limp now, loose and limp. All tension, all concern disappears. The light somehow seems to dissipate all negative energy and wash away any worry or concern.*

So I'm safe and comfortable but still quite aware of my surroundings. And this is ever more peaceful and ever more pleasant. Relax, relax. I let the light move down to my chest and lungs now, let it fill my being with peace and health. I allow it to saturate every muscle, nerve, and fiber of my being; and I recognize it as it happens. For I symbolically acknowledge this wonderful state of letting go even more, and thereby going deeper and deeper. Deeper and deeper I go into the innermost sanctuary of my being, and it feels so good. I breathe deeply for a moment. I feel my breath fill my lungs and hold that breath to the mental count of three.

I let it go slowly, counting mentally from one to three. Here I go. Breathe in . . . one . . . two . . . three . . . hold . . . one . . . two . . . three . . . breathe out . . . one . . . two . . . three . . . hold . . . one . . . two . . . three . . . While doing this three more times, I find myself going into an even deeper and more peaceful state, a place in my mind that is so tranquil that I will want to return here often.

Okay, I let the light work its way down to the tip of my toes, the very tips of my toes. I feel it moving down, and I can guide it the rest of the way. I guide it right out to the very tip of each toe. As I do this, I continue deepening my relaxation. Now my unconscious mind knows exactly what to do.

My deepest memories, all I have ever learned and much more, are stored away in that vast reservoir of knowledge and wisdom known as the unconscious or subconscious mind. From here on out, my conscious mind can continue to work the light all the way down and right on out through the tips of my toes. Continuing to breathe slowly and deeply as the light fully fills all of my being, I acknowledge the success my conscious mind has achieved, and I let it rest with gratitude for the work it has done and all that it has accomplished.

I am now gaining the ability to use my own mind in its fullest potential. The thin wall between the conscious and subconscious is becoming thinner. Soon every helpful possibility that both levels of awareness can bring to any situation will be mine. All of this simply amazes me. But for now, my subconscious mind will help me achieve my goal. And if I fall asleep before I come to the end of this session, that is perfectly okay because my subconscious will simply continue with the work, giving me my answers in my dreams. . . .

Helpful Tip

Use an InnerTalk subliminal program or your own custom one (full instructions are given in Chapter 10) in the background to prime your self-talk with the mental language that accompanies your goal. Use this program when you sleep, while you're driving, in the background behind any television you might watch, and at any other time possible;

and for sure use one behind your self-hypnosis sessions. However, always remember to take into consideration the affirmations on the program you're working with, since some wouldn't be appropriate—in fact, they would be extremely dangerous if used in certain situations. For example, it would be absolutely contraindicated to use *I sleep well* while driving or operating machinery.

Bringing It All Together

We've now covered the five stages of hypnosis and have looked at several exercises you can use while in the hypnotic state to advance your personal growth. It's important to practice all five stages in their entirety and in the correct order (pre-relaxation, induction, deepening, utilizing, and coming back). As I stated earlier, with practice you'll be able to recognize when you've fully accomplished each step and will then be able to reach your desired state a lot faster. If you shortchange this practice period, you'll only be hurting yourself!

Once you've mastered the self-hypnosis basics, there's a great deal more that you can do. You'll learn some of these advanced techniques in the next chapter.

CHAPTER SEVEN

Further Uses of Hypnosis

"Excellence, then, is a state concerned with choice, lying in a mean relative to us, this being determined by reason and in the way in which the man of practical wisdom would determine it."

— Aristotle

Everything that you have learned in this book is now available to you to do for yourself. You can take that journey back to the innermost center of your being without any assistance. You can reproduce a progressive relaxation without any additional help. You can even create your own double binds and metaphors to assist in deepening your experience even more.

As you've seen, there are many things you can do with self-hypnosis. You can visualize yourself being successful, and there's a great deal of research that supports this use. Dr. Judd Biasiotto conducted a study at the University of Chicago to find out how visualization can affect the free-throw skills of basketball players. The players were all tested to determine their free-throw proficiency, and then they were split into three random groups.

The first group practiced shooting free throws every day for one hour. The second group didn't practice; they just visualized themselves shooting free throws accurately. The third group did nothing. After 30 days, the three groups were again tested on their free-throw shooting skills. The group that did nothing showed no improvement; in fact, many of them showed deterioration. The group that practiced one hour each day improved by 24 percent. But the second group, the one that visualized but didn't physically practice basketball, improved by 23 percent!

Related to achieving goals, self-hypnosis can be used for accessing information about yourself. Maybe you have some habit that you really want to change, but you feel you need to understand where it came from first. For this, using a variation of the Power Imaging exercise would be most effective. You can enhance and deepen a meditation with self-hypnosis, and you can also use it for connecting with your higher self.

In the next section, you're going to reverse things just a little. You're going to use some extra imagination and experience, what some call an "oceanic experience." For this exercise, which is also available on the accompanying audio download, I'll allow you to give yourself a particular cue. What will that be? Think ahead now. Perhaps you wish to remember something or you want to control some behavior, such as acting out in anger. Whatever you wish, think of it now. Remember that this is a cue to you. Make it short and all positive.

For example, let's say that you wish to remember a lot of information for an examination. The cue may be something like this: *Everything I need to know flows freely through my mind whenever I need it.* Building good cues is an art, and there are many books on the subject. You may want to take some extra time and think about yours before creating it.

This exercise is on Track 5 of the accompanying audio download. You should experience this first before reading through the transcript. For this exercise, you'll use the cue word *relax*. When you come back to look at the exercise, remember that you can change this cue word to be anything you wish.

Once again, use your audio download before reading the script below.

Exercise: The Oceanic Experience ≙

Okay, I'll begin by just imagining that I'm lying on a beach, a very sunny, warm beach. I can hear the surf in the background. From time to time, I note the sound from a gull flying overhead. I am warm and comfortable, so relaxed. Relax now, relax, relax. My entire body relaxes, and I go deep and deep and deeper, deeper than ever before. Deep, deep down into that special state of consciousness. Deep down, deep, deep down. Relax. And by absolute command, my post-hypnotic training has made this keyword [relax or your keyword]. This is my post-hypnotic cue for rapidly entering this deep and profound state of peace, balance, and harmony. Each time I use this word in this special way, I go deeper and deeper into hypnosis. Deeper and deeper, and I do so quicker and quicker.

It is my cue, and said by anyone else other than in the context of this program, it is just a word—that is, I may choose to accept it or not. But in this context as I speak it to myself, it is my cue to completely, totally relax all over. Sometimes it just seems like magic. Relax, totally relax, now. Breathe in through my nose, and I can smell a hint of the ocean air.

I'm on a beach and at rest, at peace with myself and the world around me. I am free to daydream. I've learned many things, and I've learned to access deeper meanings and reveal deeper insights into the way I think and the way I choose to act. From this day forward, I will have a renewed confidence in myself. I will notice that the things I've found to be stressful in the past will just sort of roll off me like water off a duck's back. I have become impervious to stress. I have my special place of balance, and I can go there anytime.

I'm at peace with myself and the world around me. Life is like a school. I've learned many things, and I can and will continue to learn more. I have entered a new era of total wisdom, and I now know what to do with my knowledge. I trust myself; I am confident and secure. I am good. I do deserve happiness, peace, balance, and harmony. From this day forth, I will find my new level of confidence generates a new enthusiasm for life and all that it holds. I have gained the ability to see things in balance. I am forgiving and forgiven. I am grateful. I am a miracle. I rest in the sun on the beach and know that all good things will come to me.

I am going to use my beach and a little extra imagination to cleanse, to wash away any self-limiting thoughts. Washing away residual fears or doubts totally restores the perfect vision of myself to me now. The sun focuses a special calm, bright white light and delivers this energy at the top of my scalp. It enters my body and flows throughout. It fills every aspect of my being. It overflows me and radiates many feet outward from my whole body and being. The cells of my body celebrate. I feel warm and protected and good in every way. A miracle has just happened. I have become one with the light, and now the ocean vapor washes over me, light vapor. And the salt in the sea cleanses all of the outer me. And I am new.

The sound of the ocean reminds me of the waters of consciousness, and I am an individual aspect of all consciousness. As a crystal clear drop of that water, my consciousness does affect and influence the total. I do make a difference, and from this day forward I take my inner glow or sense of being, my peace, balance, and harmony with me everywhere. I influence others sometimes without saying a word. I am a gift in everything that I will ever be. I accept the gift. I am a miracle. Life is glorious, and it only gets better.

I am now in touch with myself and the world around me. I take a moment. It feels so good. I take a moment to feel the bliss. I sense a peace that is so profound, it's unlike anything I've ever done.

Now I will use my post-hypnotic cue. My cue is [relax or your keyword]. This word is, by post-hypnotic command, my pathway to almost instant gratification, deep, deep down into my special state of hypnosis. So whenever I say [relax or your keyword] to myself, by absolute command I go deeply into this state of profound relaxation.

Remember, I will always have command of my faculties. I will always be alert and prepared if needed. But I use this post-hypnotic command only when I close my eyes and can go deep into hypnosis. Therefore, only when it's appropriate to close my eyes will this command work. When I use it, my eyes will close and I will go deeply and naturally very quickly into hypnosis.

Okay, it's time to return. This time I'll do that with a forward count from one to five. Upon five, my eyes will open and I will be refreshed and rested, amazed by what a few brief moments in hypnosis can do. Number one, beginning to come back now. Number two, coming back, coming back. Number three, almost there. Number four, coming back now, coming back. Number five, eyes open, eyes open. All the way back, wide awake now, wide awake now. I am feeling very, very good all over in every way . . . very, very good all over, wide awake.

The Mind as a Transceiver

Most people think of the mind as limited to the physical organ—the brain. This assumption is false. The evidence for mind beyond "organ-brain" is simply overwhelming. Everything from the paranormal to the ordinary day in and day out experiences of so-called ordinary people suggests that the mind knows things that are just out of reach, unless the mind somehow transcends the limitation of this physicality.

I like to think of the mind as a sort of transceiver. It has the ability to tune in certain stations, if you will, like a radio. It can also send, not just receive. Where all this takes place and exactly how is still unknown, but we can think of it like this: Assume a dimension that we'll call hyperspace. Now think of this hyperspace as able to contain many modulating frequencies, the way our own space-time is able to hold many different radio signals simultaneously, just at difference frequencies. In other words, take our radio dial. We could tune it to any number of stations. They're all present in the same dimension, but they typically don't interfere with each other due to differences in the frequency band used for their broadcast. In this special sense then, perhaps the mind is able to transcend space-time and enter hyperspace, where "frequencies" might exist that could be thought of as past and future. For that matter, it also makes sense to think of this non-space-time dimension—hyperspace—as a corridor that may well lead to many other alternative dimensions that physicists are certain exist simultaneously with our four-dimensional world.

Throughout recorded history, metaphysical teachers have taught that the mind can be placed in such a state that it's not only capable of controlling the body, but of leaving the body, and also doing both simultaneously. There are many mysteries, and the organ-brain is not the mind any more than the driver is the automobile. So next, we'll explore some of these mysteries and learn how to continue your personal journey in whatever area you choose. There was a time that education focused more on doing and less on theory. One became a carpenter by working wood, not by simply reading about it in books. We're going to approach today's learning from that standpoint.

Exploring with the Mind

Let's begin by looking at out-of-body awareness. You can think of this as remote viewing or astral-travel training—whatever you're comfortable with. The idea of this session is to illustrate through experience what the mind outside of the body might be like.

Exercise: Out-of-Body Awareness ≙

Instructions: Get comfortable, and let's take a trip in the vehicle we call the mind. This exercise is on the accompanying audio download (Track 6), and I again encourage you to experience the audio program first and then come back and look at the following script.

I just let go now and relax. Relax, relax, relax. I close my eyes, relax, feel the quietness of spirit enter and fill my being right down to the tips of my toes. Think, Relax, relax, relax, *and all of that relaxation I knew during my last hypnosis session just permeates my entire being. Calm and relaxed. Nothing to do, relax, relax all over. Totally and wholly relaxed. I just think,* Relax, *and let go. Let go all over.*

Now, to assist myself in knowing still deeper states of relaxation, I feel myself descending right down into the center of my being, like a journey to the center of the Earth. Slowly descending as in a hot air balloon, I am safe, comfortable, warm, protected. I'm going right down into the center of my being where my inner light dwells. It's not a place, per se, it's a state of mind or a state of being. Still, all of my consciousness moves there now, and as it does, my entire body goes loose and limp and flaccid.

I am relaxed, all over, loose and limp and flaccid. Nothing matters but my journey to the center of my being. In the center of my being is all the wisdom of the universe. Here I can find answers that otherwise evade me. Here I can know things that are otherwise unknowable. Here only a part of me is in space-time. But even that part is not of space-time at this point. It's more than a magical moment—it's who I really am. My quintessential pure self dwells in the center of my being, and all of my higher powers are there to be awakened or remembered as I would have it. Descending slowly, I count down now from ten to one. By the time I reach one, I will have arrived safe, comfortable, and even a little excited about what I will find, for treasures await me in this magical place.

Ten, going down slowly now, descending down, comfortably down, down, down. Nine, further down now, sinking into the center of my being, down, down, down. As I descend, something unexpected occurs. I begin to become expanded in awareness, although in a very special way. It's as if my mental abilities are literally doubling with each count. I am able to hold more and more information at the same time, but without stress or tension of any kind. Images and thoughts begin to bind together in unique ways. This provides a new perspective on almost everything.

Eight, going deeper and deeper.

Seven, continuing down to the center of my being while simultaneously experiencing new insights and a special expanded sense of awareness that will reinforce a new expanded sense of self-confidence. Six, by the time I get there, I will be so totally relaxed and yet so totally expanded in awareness that I will sense an absolutely unshakable level of confidence in myself and in my abilities.

Five, halfway there, I'm going still deeper and deeper and deeper, way down deep now, way down deep. Four, soon I will be at the deepest level possible for me at this time . . . deep, deep down within myself . . . peaceful, calm, tranquil, serene, and it feels so good all over. Three, almost there now, deep, deep, deeper still, way, way down within my own being . . . deep, deep, down.

Two, continuing to descend—descend, and very soon I will arrive, safe, secure, calm, so deeply relaxed that nothing matters but my awareness. So able to contain what seems like the entire universe at one time, it's amazing. I am a being of almost pure energy, and my thoughts are free to travel, and the speed of thought is much faster than the speed of light.

Free, without barriers, and I am almost to the center of my being where every power that resides within me will become me, for it is me after all. And one, I'm there now at the center of my being.

I look around. There's a portal resembling a small window on an airplane. I go to that portal and look through it. Just on the other side is non-space-time. This is my portal to hyperspace. I can create many wonderful things there, and they will materialize in normal space-time if my intent is pure, and it is in everyone's highest best interest. I'm going to pass through that portal and then back into space-time in such a novel way that I will find this exercise totally empowering.

By simply thinking myself through the portal, I enter hyperspace. I do so now. Swirling peaceful colors of light, bands of geometry, and a boundless sense of self and energy abide here now. I think of myself in space-time on planet Earth in a past lifetime. It's not important whether I believe in past lives; I just let myself be a visitor if nothing else. I'm either entering space-time in a prior life or visiting space-time on Earth anytime in the past 500 years. I think it and make it happen and make it real with the unlimited power of my mind. I will count to three and when I reach three, I will be there and the images will be clear. Number one, number two, number three. I'm there now.

What do I see? I take a moment and look around. Where am I? What am I doing? Is there anyone near? Is this a memory of something I've lived, or am I visiting? I take a few moments alone to become familiar with where I am. I am safe and secure, but should I encounter something that in any way disturbs me, I will simply open my eyes and end this session. Otherwise, I take the time now to explore this past life. [Pause]

Okay, it's time to return. I'll do this with a forward count from one to five. Upon five, my eyes will open, and I'll feel fresh and rested, feeling good now in every way; good all over. I remember and return with all that I have gained during this session. Okay, number one, beginning to return to that ordinary state of consciousness. Number two, coming back now; and even though it's natural to want to go deeper and stay longer, I'll be fully back by the time I reach five. Number three, coming back, coming back; each time I go into this state, I go quicker and deeper in my special sense of deep relaxation.

My post-hypnotic cue to enter this state is [relax or your keyword], and whenever I use that word, I will go deep, deep, deep into this profound state of relaxation . . . deep, deep, deep into hypnosis. Number four, soon I'll be fully back, fully back; and everything that I have experienced I will remember, and it will empower me more and more each day. All right, number five, fully back now, fully back, eyes open, eyes open, wide awake, wide awake and feeling good all over in every way, wide awake. I am at peace with myself.

Think about what you just learned and experienced. Where is the line between real and imagined? Did you learn anything about yourself? Pause and reflect for a few moments, perhaps even a day before continuing.

And Beyond

By now you have a good idea of just what you might be able to do with your new self-hypnosis tools. Here are a few more scripts that you can utilize within your self-hypnosis session.

Exercise: Regression Therapy

Instructions: Start with your pre-relaxation, induction, and deepening. This exercise picks up right where the final deepening part ends.

Now, I wish to find the cause of my particular problem. I am aware that this is rooted somewhere in my past, and I know that my subconscious holds this information. But now I am deeply relaxed, and I know that I am perfectly safe, that no matter what I learn, I will see things as though they are occurring to someone else. All the emotions from the event will remain in the past. It is just the memory that will filter through, just the memories I need in order to move beyond this.

In front of me I see a hallway. There are doors lining one side of this hallway, and on each door is a number. The door closest to me has the number of my current age. As I walk down the hallway, I count the numbers on the doors (50 . . . 49 . . . 48 . . . 47 . . .). My subconscious mind will let me know which door will lead me to the information that I seek (46 . . . 45 . . . 44 . . .).

An inner knowing tells me when I have reached the correct door. Feeling perfectly safe, knowing I am perfectly safe and calm, I reach forward and open the door. Once it is open, I see a screen on the far wall. On this screen is the information I am seeking. I look at the screen and instantly I remember . . .

When I am through watching the screen, I exit the room and close the door. Instantly I am back in my place of pure calm, peaceful relaxation. I can choose to stay here, or I can choose to come out of this hypnosis session. I know when the time is right, and I begin my exit process . . .

From Mind to Hand

Self-hypnosis can also be used for automatic writing or drawing. It does take quite a bit of practice, so don't be disheartened if you don't achieve it right away. Simply continue to practice all the other techniques I've taught you in this book. When you're ready, you can use the following script. You will, of course, need to conduct this hypnosis session in a position that is conducive to writing and have paper, a pen, and a flat surface all prepared. Maybe you'll want to sit in a comfortable chair, semi-reclined, with a pad of paper and pencil in your lap.

Exercise: Automatic Writing/Drawing

Instructions: Start with your pre-relaxation, induction, and deepening. This exercise picks up right when the final deepening part ends.

Feeling perfectly calm and relaxed, I reach for my pen and paper. I know that the answers I am seeking are in my subconscious, and I will use my pen and paper to access this information easily. I feel the pen in my hand. I do not need to open my eyes, but I can if I wish. It is all up to me. I keep my attention focused simply on staying nice and calm and relaxed, enjoying the peace and tranquility that comes from this place.

I am aware of my pen moving across the paper, and even this action assists me in remaining calm and relaxed. My hand is perfectly comfortable, and it feels very normal for me to be writing this way. I allow the process just to unfold.

When my subconscious is finished giving me this information, I allow the pen to fall from my hand, and I sink back deeper and deeper into relaxation.

In just a few moments, I know my subconscious mind will allow me to decipher what I have written or drawn. Feeling more and more relaxed, I count to five, knowing that when I reach the count of five, my eyes will open, I will see my paper, and I will instantly understand what my subconscious is telling me.

One . . . two . . . three . . . four . . . five. My eyes open, and I see the paper. I know exactly what it means, but there are no emotions attached to the memory. After a few moments, I close my eyes and go back into my safe, serene place of complete relaxation.

I then begin my exit out of hypnosis . . .

Further Applications

There really are no limits to what you can do with hypnosis. You can use the Regression Therapy exercise in this chapter to examine your past. You can even play with it and try the technique going forward.

For the more practically minded, hypnosis has been deemed a powerful facilitator in areas as diverse as habit control, such as smoking and drinking, and irritable bowel syndrome. Probably the best-known uses are for weight loss, relaxation, and entertainment purposes. That said, here is a short list of conditions that medical professionals have found treatable with hypnosis:

- Addictions
- Alopecia areata
- Asthma
- Bed-wetting
- Cancer-related pain
- Eating disorders
- Fibromyalgia
- Indigestion (dyspepsia)
- Insomnia
- Irritable bowel syndrome
- Labor and delivery
- Pain management
- Phobias

- Skin disorders, such as acne, psoriasis, and eczema (atopic dermatitis)
- Stress
- Tension headaches
- Tinnitus (ringing in the ears)
- Warts
- Weight loss

Here's just a partial list of areas for which professional hypnotherapists and hypno-technicians, together with hypnosis researchers, might use hypnosis:

- Athletics
- Bed-wetting
- Behavior therapy
- Blood-sugar management
- Body image
- Bruxism
- Dating
- Fear reduction
- Female breast enlargement

- Forensic applications
- Forgiveness
- Grief
- Hair pulling
- Immune strengthening
- Learning
- Memory/recall
- Nail biting
- Past-life regression
- Public speaking
- Regression work
- Self-confidence
- Self-healing
- Sex enhancement
- Sleep
- Snoring
- Spirituality
- Stomach upsets
- Stuttering

I could go on to list perhaps another 200 or so areas. This list exists only to open your eyes to the horizon of possibilities. In other words, once you've conditioned yourself to enter self-hypnosis, the sky seems to be the limit.

One more note: As you can see, this collection is just an introduction. You have learned to do self-hypnosis, but that's just a tool. What you do with the tool is your next step. If you use it only to relax and still your thoughts, you'll be far ahead of most.

Not only does this feel good, it is, as your mom might have said, "good for you." If you choose to pursue hypnosis further, I suggest that you advance your skills by studying the work of Dr. Milton Erickson. He was simply the best, and the majority of today's practitioners use many of his techniques.

And don't forget, I've created a special InnerTalk program to enhance your abilities in learning self-hypnosis. Simply go to **www.eldontaylor.com/HypnosisAndSubliminal** and download your copy now.

PART III

SUBLIMINAL COMMUNICATION

CHAPTER EIGHT

SUBLIMINAL COMMUNICATION: A BRIEF OVERVIEW

*"The mind is its own place, and in itself
can make a heaven of Hell, a hell of Heaven."*

— JOHN MILTON

In a number of different surveys, carried out at different times over the last 25 years, the consensus of the public is that:

1. Subliminal communication is real.
2. Subliminal messages ("subliminals") are being used—in the media, in entertainment, and in politics.
3. Subliminals don't work.
4. The public is protected from the misuse of subliminals.
5. Subliminals are dangerous.

I don't know about you, but for me these views appear to be totally dissonant. How can this information be dangerous but not work? How can the public be protected from the misuse of subliminals if they're still being employed by so many?

This is a very large issue, which I've covered in detail in a number of my earlier books (most recently *Mind Programming* and *Choices and Illusions*). However, I do believe it's important to at least review the most salient points here, as it will assist you in gaining a much better understanding of why I consider this, along with self-hypnosis, to be the most valuable, effective, and affordable of self-help technologies.

History

The popular history of information processing without awareness, sometimes called "shadowed," "masked," or "peripheral" information, but commonly known by the public under one general label as subliminal communication, is really a history of modern manipulation.

Various forms of subliminal stimuli and their influence on the individual have been evaluated since the late 19th century, and there was little dispute in scientific circles regarding subliminal-information processing per se. The majority of disagreements among scientists were about how much influence a stimulus could have, how much behavior could be shaped or guided, how long the stimulus effect might last, and so forth. Fundamentally—and this is the important point—the general consensus was that subliminal information (stimulus of an audio, visual, or kinesthetic type) was processed and could predispose both thought and action based on the nature of the stimulus.

Are We Being Manipulated?

Subliminal communication really came to the public's attention with the release of Vance Packard's work *The Hidden Persuaders* in 1957. Although discredited by many, by the late 1960s this book had made it onto the required-reading list for many high schools. Packard quoted from *The Sunday Times* of London regarding an account of a New Jersey theater where ice-cream ads were flashed onto the screen during a movie, resulting in claims of an otherwise unaccountable increase in ice-cream sales. The paper referred to this technique as "sub-threshold effects."[1] As a result of investigations, James Vicary (the market researcher allegedly in charge of this experiment) denied ever conducting the popcorn, cola, and ice-cream trials in his theater. Whether he actually did or not has never been proven. We do know that he had the ability to do so, but perhaps he only made the claim to sell the equipment that his company, Precon Processing, built.

Packard's work warned of psychologists turned merchandisers and of the resulting psycho-seduction of the American consumer. From belief systems to product identification, he presented a case for persuasion through the art and science of motivational analysis, feedback, and psychological manipulation. *Hidden Persuaders* was the first open attempt to inform the general public of a potentially Orwellian means to surreptitiously enslave the mind.

In his books *Subliminal Seduction* and *Clam-Plate Orgy,* Wilson Brian Key argued that not only are we being bombarded with subliminal advertising today, but the public has been subliminally seduced for hundreds of years. Key, a Canadian university professor, sums it all up in the title to a third book on the subject: *Media Sexploitation.*[2]

According to Professor Benjamin Wolman, subliminal research is at least as old as M. Suslowa's work in 1863 wherein he reported "an increase in the two-point discrimination threshold as a function of subliminal electrical stimulation."[3] In 1894 W. R. Dunham, M.D., wrote an interesting commentary on the subliminal mind and subliminal communication. Nearly 100 years later, Dunham's essay reads much like current research on the subject. In his article "The Science of Vital Force," Dunham demonstrated the existence of both the subliminal mind and subliminal communication.[4]

One of Sigmund Freud's most important contributions to approaching the enigma known as the human condition was the stark revelation that humankind is a mere particle of its potential. Unconscious processes predetermine conscious choices and, therefore, behavior. Aggregates of attitude and behavior constitute personality, which is rather rigid. Consequently, the human condition is an abysmal shadow of itself. What's more, according to Freud, it's inherently in conflict with itself.[5]

A contemporary of Freud's, Dr. O. Poetzle, studied subliminal perception under exact laboratory conditions and discovered behavior effects days and weeks following the presentation of the original stimuli.[6]

Wolman's modified categorization of subliminal stimuli divides descriptive values into four criteria of awareness and unawareness. The stimulus is one of the following:

1. Below the level of registration
2. Above the level of registration but below the level of detection
3. Above the level of detection and discrimination but below the level of identification
4. Below the level of identification only because of a defensive action[7]

Using Wolman's categories, the patented subliminal technology known as InnerTalk (which I'll cover more in the next chapter) falls in the third category. Wolman makes several general statements regarding subliminal stimulation, having come to certain conclusions based upon his erudite research. Although maintaining a cautious stance, he asserts:

1. Subliminal stimulus does leave an influence upon the content of subsequent cognition.

2. Subliminal stimuli have affected and can affect secondary process thinking.
3. There are neurophysiologic findings that appear to concur with registration without awareness.
4. Despite some failures of replication, there are numerous instances where subliminal stimuli "can measurably influence a variety of subject's subsequent behaviors."
5. Conscious thinking can be influenced by stimuli outside of awareness.[8]

In 1981, Dr. Norman Dixon summarized more than 748 references on subliminal stimulation in his scholarly book *Preconscious Processing.* Dixon provides a model for understanding the flow of information and its entry to consciousness. According to his model, five factors govern whether a stimulus surfaces at a conscious level: direction of attention, signal strength, external noise level, internal noise level, and signal importance (meaning).[9]

The Law and Informed Consent

Most people assume that laws are in force to protect them against the misuse of subliminal communication. Unfortunately, that's not the case. Part of the reason for the absence of laws rests with confusion about definitions. In the 1984 congressional hearings on the matter, the only real consensus that was reached implied that any law written would have to approach the matter from a standpoint of "informed consent."[10]

Not long after the hearings before the U.S. House of Representatives Committee on Science and Technology, an informed-consent law was introduced in Utah. In 1986, Representative Frances Merrill of the Utah House of Representatives initiated legislation to prohibit subliminal communication without informed consent. In other words, just as restaurants used to be required to post notices regarding microwave use, a retailer using antitheft "subliminals," for example, would be required to inform those who might hear the audio programs. Obviously, heavy-metal-music groups using subliminals would also be required to display appropriate notices, as would all other users of such communication.

I was involved in this legislative process, as was my business. I cohosted a radio talk show at the time, and my staff and I took the argument to the airwaves. In my opinion, not only did an informed-consent law make sense, but it appeared then and now to be the only legal measure likely to be enforceable and not infringe on constitutional freedoms. Perhaps I shouldn't have been as surprised as I was on the day we addressed the Utah House committee, but I recall being almost shocked by the number of professionals representing various interests, including advertising agencies, who showed up to speak against the legislation. What we thought was a local decision apparently had national and even international interest. Speakers from New York argued that the legislation wasn't needed—no one used this technology, it was too expensive, and it didn't work. The committee heard both sides and was pressed by my office and others to at least send the issue to the full House for a vote.

The committee narrowly approved the proposed legislation to go to the House floor, but it was never presented for a vote on the floor and as such died. To this date, although several states and even the United States Congress have introduced legislation to prohibit subliminal information in public-communication media, no legislation has ever been enacted.

The FCC

A Federal Communications Commission (FCC) codification does prohibit subliminal content. It essentially is a warning to broadcasters (technically the FCC could pull a broadcaster's license for violation), but then there's the whole matter of discovery. For example, when television stations broadcast a toy advertisement with subliminal messages that were delivered slightly out of sync, the hidden directive became obvious: "Tell Mom, buy now." Concerned citizens complained, but everyone denied creating this message.

Without the power of discovery, where to next? In other words, without a punitive description in a penal code, it all comes down to cooperation. What technically might be pursued and what practically is pursued are generally not the same. We do know that in the case of the ad just mentioned, nothing happened.

The Controversy

With so much research having been done on subliminal communication, you may be wondering why this technology is so controversial. I've alluded to part of this in the section above—big business, the advertising industry, and the entertainment industry all have a vested interest in convincing the public that this technology doesn't work, just so that they can continue using it! Also, a number of personalities, including Madonna, have deliberately used subliminal information in their works, releasing the fact that it was included and benefitting from the subsequent publicity.

However, it was really the Judas Priest trial in Reno, Nevada, that had the greatest impact on the public's perception and understanding of subliminal information processing. Again, this is covered in detail in my book *Mind Programming,* but I will summarize the information for you here.

The Judas Priest Trial

In 1990, the now-infamous Judas Priest wrongful death action in Reno, Nevada, asserted in part that subliminal stimuli in the heavy metal band's *Stained Class* album were a causal factor in the deaths of two young men who shot themselves. The subliminal command "Do it" had been found on a track with lyrics that overtly encouraged suicide, and this song had been played repeatedly just before the boys went out and attempted to commit suicide. One was immediately successful; the other shot off the front of his face and died three years later.

There was a long and very public trial, but it can be difficult for an ordinary family to fight a mega corporation like CBS. However, at the conclusion of the trial, the judge learned that CBS had, at great expense, manipulated the media before and during the trial. It released continuous press packages through a publicity and public-relations firm. Such firms and such packages have a simple purpose: to control public opinions. The judge warned CBS on the morning of his verdict that, "The court will be investigating this action, since some of the material given in press releases is totally improper and could constitute slander." He then fined CBS $40,000 for impeding the discovery process and not bringing forward the original music track master. CBS had failed to produce the original 24-track music master for analysis, saying that they could not find it. This was in spite of hiring a former Scotland Yard detective to search high and low for the master. The detective, however, told the court under oath that he hadn't been allowed to look in the vaults!

The trial ended, and the media repeated reporting about the absolute waste of taxpayers' money spent on such a foolish issue. Newspapers and magazines around the world received media packages scoffing at the entire concept of subliminal perception. Large-dollar advertisers sent slanted information to the press and placed advertising if the copy was accepted for print. Experts for CBS began speaking out. They argued that subliminal information processing didn't exist except as a subject for laughter, and that it depended on the foolish idea of a smart subconscious mind able to receive and process this data.

The Spangenberg Study

One of the studies, touted at the time for disproving the subliminal effect, was carried out by Eric Spangenberg.[11] In this study, he set up a research project using subliminal audiotapes from five different companies. There were two kinds of tapes, one to improve memory and one to build esteem. The labels were switched, however, so that the esteem tapes were labeled "Memory," and vice versa. After the testing period, subjects were evaluated for actual improvement. Those who thought they were playing memory subliminal messages reported an improvement in memory, and those who believed they were listening to esteem messages reported an increase in esteem. The instruments failed to identify a statistically meaningful change in either. It's fair enough, at this point, to state a definite label influence, but how about a real effect regarding subliminal communication?

The five tape companies all claimed different methods and messages for their programs, including messages in both the second person and first person. Audio analysis failed to recover messages on any of the programs. Some companies used questionable affirmations and in other ways produced material that differentiated one product from another. All shared the label "subliminal," but that certainly didn't mean they were the same. So we're not looking at a scientific study with a single variable. We're mixing multiple variables and coming up with a single conclusion—and that simply isn't good science!

First Amendment Violation

Despite all this, the wrongful death action brought against Judas Priest and CBS in Reno led to a judicial interpretation regarding subliminal communication and First Amendment rights. The Honorable Jerry Carr Whitehead (District Judge in the State of Nevada), who presided over the Judas Priest trial, ruled that it was a First Amendment violation to use subliminal information without consent.[12]

Recent Research

Whatever ultimate interpretations or direction of the controversy, one thing is quite certain, subliminals are here to stay. But with all of this controversy, it can be very easy to disregard the abundant proof of its efficacy, based on the belief that the research was done a long time ago and must have since been disproven. However, this is not the case, for much research has been done in recent years, and more is being done all the time. I will not go into all the studies, but to give you a taste, let me cite just a few.

In 2007, the findings of cognitive neuroscientist Ken Paller at Northwestern University demonstrated that facial expressions that aren't noticed consciously do register subliminally. In the words of Paller's colleague Wen Li, as quoted by Charles Choi in *Live Science:* "Our results show that an unconsciously perceived signal of threat, such as a brief facial expression of fear, can still bubble up and unwittingly influence social judgments and how we act."[13]

According to an article that appeared in *New Scientist* and was posted on **NewScientist.com**, Johan Karremans of the University of Nijmegen in the Netherlands subliminally induced subjects to like a particular drink. Karremans used both thirsty and what one might call regular-thirst subjects and flashed before them the 23-millisecond subliminal message "Lipton Ice." When later asked to choose a drink, both groups significantly favored the Lipton Ice brand beverage; and of the thirsty group, 80 percent chose Lipton Ice. This outcome suggests that the presence of the subliminal message is made stronger or acted upon sooner by a congruent drive (thirst).[14]

A CBC News report from Ontario, Canada, appearing on February 26, 2007, announced the removal of slot machines that allegedly flashed subliminal winning images: "The games flashed winning jackpot symbols at players for a fifth of a second, long enough for the brain to detect even if the players are not aware of the message, some psychologists told CBC News." The company Konami, which produces the slots, claims it's clearly only a "software glitch." CBC News added, "Problem gamblers complain that the machines affect how they think, electronic gaming specialist Horbay said. They can't pinpoint the problem, but 'this may be a part of what they believe is messing up their heads.'"[15]

Researchers at the University of Jerusalem also tested the subliminal impact of flags as symbols. They reported their findings in the *Proceedings of the National Academy of Sciences* in 2007. They found the subliminal "presentation of the Israeli flag was sufficient to make people adopt more moderate views."[16]

Headlines everywhere in March 2008 touted the almost magical effect the Apple logo had on creativity. Professors Gavan Fitzsimmons and Tanya Chartrand of Duke University joined with Grainne Fitzsimmons of Waterloo University, Canada, in this experiment. Subjects were presented subliminally with either the IBM or the Apple logo (the rainbow version) to test the influence of both on creativity. The researchers assumed—correctly—that the Apple logo would have more creative impact because of the brand's association with creativity. In an *Information Week* article, author Thomas Claburn noted: "The findings are sure to spark a resurgence of interest in subliminal marketing because a follow-up test showed that imperceptible exposure to other well-known brands also produced a response in subjects. When shown the Disney channel logo, for example, participants behaved more honestly than those shown the E! Channel logo."[17] (A resurgence? As if the merchandisers had ever stopped using subliminal technology!)

In the UK, a team of researchers from University College in London used brain scans—visual images and functional MRIs—to watch subliminal information as it was processed by their seven subjects. They observed activity in the primary visual cortex when delivering the subliminal information under "easy task" terms (such as picking out the letter *H* from a list of letters). However, they found that in circumstances defined as "more difficult," the findings weren't as pronounced. The article then pointed out that subliminal advertising was banned in the UK but is still permitted in the United States. It closed with comments that essentially assert the following: Okay, now we have absolute physical proof that subliminal messages are processed in the brain—but that doesn't mean they'll influence behavior. [18] (Really, now—do you believe that?)

In two studies carried out in 2000 and 2003, researchers found that sexual response may be caused by unconscious cognitive processing. This may suggest an extra power of the unconscious nature of information processing where subliminal stimuli are concerned. If so, it would only bear out what the ad agencies' research apparently discovered long ago. According to researchers writing for the *Journal of Sex Research,* "In men, subliminally presented sexual primes facilitated recognition of sexual targets. Without the need of conscious evaluation, sexually competent stimuli activated sexual implicit memory and set up sexual responding."[19] In nonspecialist language, the researchers found that the subliminal presentation of, say, a woman's breast resulted in a sexual response in men.

The study tested the female response to subliminal stimuli as well. The findings were somewhat different, as was the conclusion drawn by the researchers: "It is possible that although implicit information processing is qualitatively similar for women and men, there is a quantitative difference. Men do seem to be more strongly motivated sexually than women." [20]

In 2009, Rosellina Ferraro (University of Maryland), James R. Bettman, and Tanya L. Chartrand (both of Duke University) published a paper regarding a series of experiments using Dasani water. They reported that study participants who looked at pictures of people near bottles of Dasani were more likely to choose that brand over three others—even if they didn't know they'd seen the logo.[21]

Recent Uses

As we've seen, subliminals have been used in advertising since at least the 1950s, but following are a few examples of some more recent uses.

In February 2008, Channel Ten in Australia was investigated for allegedly using subliminal advertising during a music-awards program. Purportedly, "during the October telecast, frames of sponsor logos lasting 1⁄25 of a second (standard visual subliminal time frame) flashed onto the screen part of the way through each award category. The logos of the programs sponsors—Chupa Chups, KFC, Toyota, BigPond and Olay—also topped and tailed each segment."[22] At this juncture, it's easy to see the advantage that advertisers seek in doing this.

In the 2000 Presidential elections, there was a great outcry over a Republican commercial that was found to contain the subliminal word *RATS* over Al Gore's face. Many explanations were given, ranging from "It was an accident" to "The RATS was just the tail end of the word DEMOCRATS." The whole incident was made much more of a joke when George

Bush wasn't even able to say the word subliminal correctly, and the entire matter was put to bed by a comment that went something like: "What's the big deal? It was only one frame of the entire commercial!"

You may be interested to know that during the same time frame, I was approached by a representative of a prominent politician from another country and asked about the use of a subliminal advertisement. After some discussion, I advised the politician to employ subliminal messaging only if the audience was informed. The campaign could use the technique to get attention and place the subliminal message "Be sure to vote" in the ad. This text only encouraged voting, not choosing a specific candidate. The politician chose not to use any subliminal content, or at least not to have my assistance in creating such a program.

But back to the RATS ad, which was selling a President—or selling away from a candidate, if you prefer to see it that way. A follow-up study was conducted to determine how effective the TV spot may have been. Psychologist Joel Weinberger from Adelphi University in Garden City, New York, and his colleague Drew Westen of Emory University in Atlanta, developed a questionnaire, which they placed on a website. In it, they asked visitors to evaluate potential candidates from their pictures. The experimenters flashed one of four sets of letters on the purported candidate's face: RATS, STAR, ARAB, and XXXX. Subjects were divided into groups by the letter set they received subliminally.

Sid Perkins reported on this study in *Science News Online* in an article titled, "Dirty Rats: Campaign Ad May Have Swayed Voters Subliminally."

He stated, "Exposure to RATS had the same negative effect among men and women in the study. In addition, participants who identified themselves as Republicans responded to RATS just as negatively as Democrats did." Further, this study showed that the subliminal influence was stronger when statements that accompanied the candidate's photo were negative.[23]

During the 2008 Presidential election, KMSP, a Fox Television affiliate in Minneapolis/St. Paul, showed Barack Obama's face in the background during the story of a terrorist sex offender. The station claims it was some sort of mistake. Also, pictures of John McCain and his wife, Cindy, were recently found embedded in the Fox News logo. In my opinion, this combination of images can't be an accident—rather, each case is a clear example of subliminal priming. Take a look for yourself and see if you agree. Go to **www.youtube.com**, and search for "Who's That Hiding In My Fox 5 News Logo?" In fact, while you're there, do a search for subliminal ads—I'm sure you will be amazed by how frequently subliminal messages are being hidden in the television programming you watch every day!

What Can We Conclude from This?

By now, it should be very clear to you that subliminal communication does in fact work, that research continues to demonstrate its efficacy, and that this technology is being used against you, not only to enhance your entertainment, but also to control your decision-making mechanisms.

However, while this information may be of great importance and worthy of public outcry, what does any of this have to do with self-improvement and personal empowerment? We'll answer this question next.

CHAPTER NINE

Subliminal Technology as a Self-Help Modality

"If the grace of God miraculously operates, it probably operates through the subliminal door."

— William James

While the history of subliminal communication is fascinating, once again I need to come back to the purpose of this book and show you the practical applications of this technology. Perhaps the easiest way to do this is to tell you how I first used it and the results I found.

My Introduction to Subliminals

In the early 1980s, I heard that the Los Angeles Police Department had experimented with subliminal programs for a terrorist-abduction scenario as part of their preparation for the Olympic Games to be hosted in L.A. The idea was a simple one. Because so much time is typically spent in negotiations over the phone, the subliminal messages would suggest illness. The masking sound was supposedly that of a furnace, or what is known as "pink noise." I was told that the police department tested this program and then suspended it after three days because it was dehydrating cadets. I have never been able to either find confirmation or denial for this report, so I don't honestly know if it was done or not. What I do know is the story was the beginning of my interest in subliminal communication.

My business at the time was criminalistics. I owned an agency that, among other things, ran several hundred lie-detection tests a year. One of the problems encountered in deception testing is known as "inconclusives." That is, the charts are not clear enough to say with confidence that deception is indicated or that the test is nondeceptive. Inconclusives are generally the product of poor test structure and pre-interview techniques or, more commonly, countermeasures or situational stress. The long and the short of it goes this way: Honest persons are so nervous about the test results that their stress spills across all questions in such a way as to lower the net differential between relevant questions and pre-stressed, control, or irrelevant questions. Dishonest persons may employ some countermeasure like the proverbial tack in the shoe and selectively administer discomfort to themselves during relevant questions, again possibly skewing the differential. I simply thought how wonderful it would be to use a subliminal program to ease the situational stress for the honest and to heighten it for those who intended to deceive. To make a long story short, I decided to find out more about subliminal communication.

Different Subliminal Technologies

Because many companies were offering subliminal programs, I phoned a number of them. I explained who I was and asked how they made their programs. You might have thought I was asking for the secret recipe for Coca-Cola. In my opinion, companies that made so-called scientific claims were obligated to provide at least some information regarding the nature of how they prepared a program that supposedly altered behavior. No one was forthcoming. Eventually, I purchased some programs and sent them to Audio Forensic Laboratories in California for analysis. When I received the report, I knew why the matter was such a secret. The bottom line was that there *were no* subliminal messages on the tapes—any of them—at least, there was no recoverable verbal content of any kind.

It was clear that for a stimulus to affect someone, there must be sufficient signal strength. Subtract the signal strength, and everything became about as subliminal as something being said a mile away. For some this may have been satisfactory because, after all, the mind was magical and it could extract verbal messages from the ether. This notion did not work for me, however, so I went back to the drawing board.

Reviewing the literature again, I found quite a bit of good audio work on what is called "shadowing," or dichotic listening, experiments. Essentially, this type of work masks one message with another. One ear may receive random numbers for a period while the other perceives a partial story, then the partial story switches to the numbers ear and the numbers switch to the story ear. Subjects normally report hearing the story and fail to report the numbers. Sometimes random words are presented to one ear and a partial story to the other. The brain selects the words it needs to complete, or fill in, the story, which is simultaneously delivered to the opposite ear.

Utilizing all of my research, some common sense, and some intuition, I eventually put together a technique for creating a subliminal program. My new method allows for the detection of occasional speech sounds, such as someone talking softly, but the words are not consciously discriminated. The next problem I had was in designing the subliminal content. What message would minimize distress in a detection of deception examination unless the subject intended to practice deception—and then have the reverse effect? This wasn't easy, but in the end I elected to use two components: the statement "The truth shall set you free" and the entirety of Psalm 23. (Psalm 23 was used by many U.S. prisoners of war during World War II and the Korean War, according to their reports, to assuage the anxiety and stress of capture.) The results astonished me. Not only did inconclusives disappear, but confession rates soared. In fact, there were times I thought of saying, "Stop, don't tell me yet—I get paid by the hour."

Utah State Prison

I reported my findings to some of the local law-enforcement agencies and heard back that the prosecutor didn't think our using this technology was such a good idea, so we stopped. Still, now that I knew this technology could work in a lie-detection scenario, I wondered about using it to rehabilitate prison inmates. A friend of mine from the Utah State Prison staff, Lee Liston, approached me with the initial idea, and we went to work on setting up a rather extensive study. We called upon another friend, Dr. Charles McCusker, a psychometric specialist, and set up a study using the Minnesota Multiphasic Personality Inventory (MMPI), which is the clinical instrument most often used to provide an objective measure of personality. It is employed quite often in court cases and is generally deemed the most reliable instrument for personality assessment.

We used prison inmates who volunteered for the study to test messages designed to lower hostility and aggression and improve chances at rehabilitation, increase reflection, and maybe eventually even interrupt the recidivism rate. The volunteers were divided into three groups: an experimental group that would receive the subliminal messages, a placebo group that would listen to the sounds of the ocean without messages, and a control group that would do nothing. The study was to take place over 30 days, with the inmate volunteers listening to the programs a minimum of one hour a day, every day.

To undo the blame, to produce self-responsible and therefore self-empowered persons, and to move away from the anger-fear loop, we decided on three messages: *I forgive myself, I forgive all others,* and *I am forgiven*. We also included statements in the first person (using "I," not "you"), because subliminal information is processed from the inside out and becomes our words in our stream of consciousness. These affirmations were designed to build self-esteem and gratitude.

Okay, what happened with our inmate population? The program worked. The results impressed everyone. The magic bullet, forgiving, together with general affirmations of well-being, worked. The Utah State Prison officials were as pleased as I was, and they followed up by installing libraries of my subliminal programs in all of their facilities.

And me? Well, this study launched a new career path for me and marked the beginning of a new way of living. I developed my technology further, patented it, and then allowed—even encouraged—independent sources to test its efficacy for themselves. Today, researchers at numerous independent universities and institutions around the world have tested the InnerTalk subliminal technology (which was patented under the name Whole Brain®) and demonstrated it to be effective. More important to me, though, are all the thank-you letters I receive every day from grateful customers around the world who inform me how their lives have been improved using this technology. But how exactly does it work in this application?

Peripheral Perception Is Natural

Peripheral perception, shadowed or masked information—it's all subliminal technology, which is one of the most powerful techniques presently available. It can rescript the preconscious mind, stripping away negative expectations and self-doubt and replacing those destructive patterns with positive input, thereby eliciting positive changes in an effortless and natural way from the inside out.

There's nothing mysterious about all of this. Yet part of the difficulty in understanding *subliminal* rests in the word itself. A subliminal message, at least in the instance of an audio program, could be defined as a verbal stimulus perceived below the threshold of awareness. Now, the key word here is *perceive.* A whisper two blocks away is below the threshold of awareness, but it isn't perceived. In order for perception by an individual to occur, there must be sufficient stimuli to trigger a neuron in the brain.

Neurons have no neutral state. They're either off or on. Therefore, the perception level that exists and is taking place with subliminals is, in fact, a neural excitation. Without it, there exists no perception, with or without awareness.

What's It Like?

In the many lectures I've presented in the United States, Asia, and Europe, there has always been a nagging need to find an analogy that could accurately describe what occurs for the users of InnerTalk audio programs. I've worked with the construct of peripheral perception to describe the manner in which voices speaking positive affirmations to the subconscious can—and indeed do—impress the listener even though they're unaware consciously of the process.

Peripheral perception is normally thought of as that aspect of sight that borders on the fringes of how far out to the right or left side we can see. The fringe always has clarity problems. That is, we may report the ability to see an object to the side, and even slightly behind us; but the further the object moves toward the limit of vision, the less clear it becomes. This is a substantially similar process to how audio perception occurs with InnerTalk.

The fringe is known as the "threshold," and the audio threshold is established by determining the point at which the conscious mind can hear a particular sound 50 percent of the time. A threshold is that place where sometimes we hear the signal and other times we don't. With InnerTalk, this point is relative to the primary carrier, music or nature sounds. Thus, the words are sometimes audible and sometimes not. The entire message may not be understood, but the voices are acknowledged by the conscious mind. Thus, from time to time we hear the message even if we don't understand every word of it.

Similar to the limit of peripheral vision, where we see an object but without the sharpness that comes from looking directly at it, InnerTalk audio messages are sometimes heard, but without the clarity the conscious mind requires in order for it to repeat the information. Shadowing the messages, as described earlier, facilitates this.

Change . . . from the Inside Out

The comparison of peripheral vision to the audio perception of an InnerTalk stimulus continues to be effective. The analogy of what happens to users of the audio subliminal program as they listen to it was much more difficult for me until a friend and I sat down to discuss just that. As we reviewed our personal experiences with InnerTalk, it became very obvious that our benefit had been gradual and from the inside out, almost intuitive in its inner direction. Often, only when the affirmations contained on the program were reread did we have an "Aha!" that acknowledged consciously why certain aspects of our drives and emotions, and therefore behavior, had changed.

Intuitive perception is just what seems to take place when you work with a well-designed program. One day you act differently because you're thinking differently. Gentle nudges from the inner mind begin to guide one's choices. In my friend's instance, creativity became natural. New ideas and concepts just seemed to flow through him. Later he experienced successes with different programs, but they were in process substantially the same as with the first one: *I Am Creative.*

All my experiences are akin to his. At first there seems to be little noticeable change, but after a few days things just seem to have a different arrangement. One day I was afraid of public speaking, to the point that I would do almost anything, invent almost any excuse, just to avoid it. Then it seemed like the next day public speaking was tolerable, and the following day I was excited about the opportunity to share with others.

Today lectures, workshops, radio, and television are just something I do like any other activity.

What we believe in our subconscious is who and what we are! The conscious mind can only guess at what's in the subconscious, while the subconscious has every thought the conscious will ever have long before it comes to awareness. In order to change, we need to change the way we think. Speaking directly to the subconscious is what subliminal messages do. One day there simply seems to be more positive than negative information in the subconscious. Then, as that wonderful bio-computer changes old inner beliefs about ourselves and the world around us, almost magically those goals, ideals, and ambitions become ours! And it happens without doubt, without fear.

Increasing the Power of the Subliminal Technology

In a very real sense, every human being has two brains. These hemispheres are commonly referred to as the right brain and the left brain. For the vast majority of people, the left hemisphere is analytical, and the right is spatial. The left hemisphere is in charge of such things as mathematics and language skills, while the right hemisphere is the creative and emotional center. The right side is indiscriminate, while the left is the seat of logic and reason with defense mechanisms such as rationalization. Most researchers also assign conscious reasoning to the left hemisphere and subconscious learning to the right.

Whole Brain InnerTalk technology appeals to the two hemispheres appropriately, in a brain friendly manner, according to the primary hemispheric function. (See the mirror-image processing or MIP paradigm described in detail in my books *Mind Programming* and *Thinking Without Thinking*.)

The left brain, then, is interested in literal correctness, while the right is more concerned with overall associations or relationships. It's believed that the left brain views language literally and according to rules of grammar, while the right brain looks at language spatially and emotionally, tumbling the words in a process called subconscious cerebration and even perceiving the words as our eyes see the world: upside down.

Some heavy-metal music recordings have included subliminal messages (usually satanic, drug related, or sexual) for years, as I touched on in the discussion of the Judas Priest trial. These messages appeal directly to emotions, causing behavior to override reason. They're also recorded in reverse, a process known as meta-contrast or back-masking. Reversing, or playing subliminal messages backward in heavy-metal music, appears to excite emotional expressions and responses often viewed as right brain in their origin.

Reviewing the research, I developed the patented InnerTalk programs using an entirely new electronic encoding process. One of the factors I had to take into consideration was exactly how I should embed the affirmations in the primary track (music or nature). As the primary track will generally have highs and lows in the volume levels, it didn't make sense to me to have the affirmations at a constant level. Doing this could result in affirmations being lost or distorted. For example, *I am confident* could become *I am con,* with the *fident* being lost due to a louder part of the music. For this reason, I designed and created a special system where the affirmations wouldn't just be placed in the primary track; they would, in fact, track the volume of the music. All of this was included in the InnerTalk technology.

There are a number of other techniques I also incorporated to increase the efficacy of the InnerTalk programs—in fact, there were 105 aspects to the original patent submission. These included features such as recording the affirmations in the permissive and authoritarian forms: *I am good* (authoritarian), and *It's okay to be good* (permissive).

With InnerTalk, accessing the left brain on one channel are meaningfully spoken, forward-masked, permissive affirmations delivered in a round-robin manner by a male voice, a female voice, and a child's voice, as appropriate. (Research shows that individuals may respond more favorably according to their preference of male, female, or child voices.) On another channel, directive messages in the same voices are recorded in meta-contrast. Since the hemispheres are task oriented, both the left and right brains become involved according to their specialties. The channel-differentiated messages shadow each other from conscious recognition.

Simple communication practices also show that we're more likely to remember a round-robin such as "Row, Row, Row Your Boat" than a simple song, even if the song is heard many more times. The round-robin affirmations are recorded in echo reverberation, producing a "singing" effect.

All you have to do is listen; no special attention is needed. Although earphones are helpful, they aren't essential. What's necessary for making the programs work is to listen to them. The more exposure to the programs, the faster results are obtained.

Why Is Subliminal Technology Effective for Self-Help?

Let's see if a couple of models of the mind can be helpful in understanding why subliminal technology is so effective. Before examining the first model, I wish to insert one of my biases. Most behaviorists assert that there are three ways in which we learn:

1. Trial and error
2. Rote core
3. Condition-response

Condition-Response

I suggest that all learning is condition-response. Trial and error employs the obvious feedback systems of both the body and the psychology. For example, with learning as basic as that involved in walking, both the pain from falling and the emotional encouragement given during the learning process form response conditioning. Where rote memory is concerned, the stimuli intensity is directly proportional to the memory retention. The stronger the stimuli (incentive), the more favorable the learning is, at least to the point of overstimulation. After that, retention is dramatically inhibited. Stimuli-response is condition-response learning.

Dr. John Kappas has created a model of learning and behavior. He suggests that we assimilate learning either through literal and direct means or through inference, and further that most of us do so primarily in one fashion or the other, not both simultaneously. For most of us, our primary caretaker (ordinarily our mother) is responsible for our suggestibility, the way we learn (that is, literally or inferentially); and our secondary caretaker (usually our father) creates our sexuality, or the way we act out our learning (that is, emotionally or physically).[1] In a very real sense, this gives rise to the acceptance, rejection, and interpretation of the various message units we receive in our lifetime.

Since our brains are tasked by hemisphere, the synthesis of our suggestibility and sexuality often produces hemispheric dominance. Thus, we may cognitively assert something that is immediately rejected or repressed, before reaching consciousness. Whenever the logic center comes into conflict with the emotional center, the emotionally conditioned response will prevail.

Now with this model in mind, let's examine a simplified bio-computer analogy and superimpose our model upon it. Every message unit we receive in a lifetime is imprinted upon the preconscious mind. This process occurs largely without discrimination, except for the lenses of interpretation, which themselves are a direct result of our primary and secondary caretakers, and from the enculturation process in general. This provides our basis for moral-value judgments and notions of reality, together with our general aptitude regarding change or the incorporation of new ideas.

Statistically, we've all received many more negative than positive message units during maturation. Our society has no rites of passage in which we leave behind all of what I refer to as the "no-don't garbage." Consequently, as adults our garbage becomes our anchor, and our ability to navigate the seas of life is limited to our own safe and sometimes shallow waters.

For most, safe waters provide our boundaries or our self-imposed limitations, which prohibit much new experience. As an example, unless we're born to success and prosperity, we don't expect to succeed and prosper because the waters surrounding our anchor don't include any such bounty.

Behaviorally, this means we're predisposed by the preconscious, which manifests as lack of confidence, fear of failure, internalization of stress, physical ailments, rationalization, and so forth. Most, if not all, of this conditioning takes place in primitive ways as far as the function of learning and behavior are concerned. The old fight-or-flight mechanisms of our ancestors give rise to deeply impressed self-limiting behavior.

Let's attempt to examine this graphically. In the following drawing, the circle represents the total mental process.

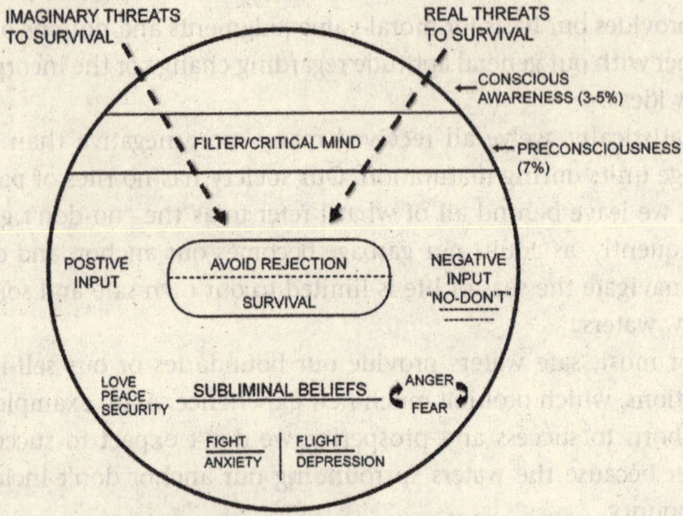

MODEL OF SUBLIMINAL PROGRAMMING

We can see the levels of consciousness, and the fight-or-flight (knee-jerk) mechanisms exist in the deepest levels. All of our input is represented by the pluses and minuses of experience (condition-response) learning. As you can see, the fight-or-flight reaction has been replaced in our modern society by anxiety and depression. The double-arrow system illustrates stimuli from the outside world, both real and synthetic, according to the interpreted emotional intensity of the stimuli.

Few of us have been presented with many real stimuli. Everything that conditions self-limiting responses is synthetic. I suggest that these stimuli are based upon an innate fear of isolation, and therefore that rejection by another human being or the fear of this happening conditions nearly all of our responses.

Our initiative and response are built upon our perception of others and our need for acceptance and understanding. Thus, behavior is purely condition-response learning! In most instances, choice is only an illusion. Only limited choices exist, and those result from the patterns of our conditioning.

The Clinical and Scientific Findings of the "Taylor Method"

As a final piece of evidence that demonstrates the effectiveness of a correctly created subliminal program in altering behavior, let me share with you some of the results of research carried out on my InnerTalk programs. As the details of every study could bog you down, I'll present only the main findings. The Endnotes have a complete list of the articles, so you may look them up yourself if you wish.

Under the direction of Dr. Jose Salvador Hernandez Gonzalez and on behalf of the Department of Social Security for Mexico, 25 patients were exposed to both video and audio *Freedom from Dental Anxiety* programs for 30 minutes prior to treatment and 30 minutes during treatment. The research reached this conclusion: ". . . the use of InnerTalk before an integral odontologic treatment is 100 percent effective, reducing patient's anxiety and the noise made by the high speed hand piece used in this type of work, and furthermore, reducing the pain suffered by comparison to previous experience." The report goes on to recommend InnerTalk: "Therefore it is convenient to promote, among Dental Surgeons, the use of InnerTalk to improve their patients comfort and achieve a better collaboration to treatments."[2]

Combining Whole Brain InnerTalk *Weight Loss* audio and video programs with an *Echo-Talk* audio program and a special nutritional program developed and marketed by Oxyfresh Worldwide, biochemical geneticist Dr. Harbans S. Sraon conducted a 90-day weight-loss study. Dr. Sraon coached subjects to visualize their clear goal in terms of body fitness and reviewed progress weekly. Dr. Sraon reported that 90 percent of the subjects (10 men and 15 women) lost significant weight.[3]

Under the direction of Maurice P. Shuman, Jr., general director for special programs of instruction, a pilot study was conducted by the Duval County Public School System at the pretrial detention center in Jacksonville, Florida. The study program included 22 incarcerated juveniles who used InnerTalk audio programs designed to assist in preparation for GED examination. The results showed that 18 of the 22 troubled students passed the full GED examination.[4]

Thomas Plante, faculty member of Stanford University and director of mental-health services for the Children's Health Council, together with Michael DiGregorio, Gerdenio Manuel, and Bao-Tran Doan of Santa Clara

University, evaluated the effect of Whole Brain InnerTalk on test anxiety in a double-blind experiment. The statistical data significantly supported the hypothesis that Whole Brain subliminal technology could be an effective tool in lowering test anxiety.[5]

Kim Roche of the University of Phoenix studied the effect of Whole Brain InnerTalk with children diagnosed as having attention deficit/hyperactivity disorder in a double-blind experiment. Her findings indicated a significant positive effect.[6]

Diana Ashley at the University of Southern California studied the effect of Whole Brain InnerTalk technology on academic achievement in a double-blind experiment. Her conclusion found a significant increase in learning among students in the experimental group.[7]

A study carried out by Professor Rainer B. Pelka of Munich University in Germany on a Whole Brain InnerTalk audio program for weight loss showed average losses of 13 pounds in subjects who used the program.[8]

The findings from a longitudinal study on the Whole Brain InnerTalk program for cancer showed that 43 percent of the patients who used the program went into remission. For the other patients, who eventually passed away, the average life span was significantly extended beyond the original prognosis.[9]

Experimental psychologist Julian Isaacs investigated the effects of the following Whole Brain InnerTalk programs: *No More Procrastination, Time Management, Confidence Power, Freedom from Stress, Positive Relationships, I Am Assertive,* and *High Self-Esteem.* After three studies, it was concluded that the programs produced significant positive results that were verifiable.[10]

A double-blind study conducted by Professor Peter Kruse of Bremen University in Germany, using a specially created Whole Brain InnerTalk program, strongly demonstrated the influence of the program on decision making. Kruse said, "The Taylor Method works!"[11]

A double-blind study was carried out at Weber State University on the effects of the Whole Brain InnerTalk program *Freedom from Stress*. The psychological test results showed a significant decrease in stress.[12]

In a double-blind study carried out at Colorado State University, it was found that using the Whole Brain InnerTalk program *Freedom from Depression* for more than 17 hours led to a significant decrease on the Beck Depression Inventory. This study not only showed the effectiveness of the Whole Brain program, but also indicated that the effectiveness of the programs was dosage related.[13]

Cosmetic surgeon Robert Youngblood and surgical staff tested the effect of the Whole Brain InnerTalk *Pre and Post Operative* audio program on 360 patients. They reported a decrease in anesthetic requirements of 32 percent by volume as compared to a historical control group.[14]

In the double-blind study at the Utah State Prison that I described earlier, performed by McCusker, Liston, and Taylor, the Whole Brain InnerTalk technology was deemed effective among inmates. As a result, the prison installed a voluntary InnerTalk audio library for inmates.[15]

Numerous clinical studies with single and multiple subjects have also found Whole Brain InnerTalk programs to be effective in areas as diverse as anorexia and dyslexia. Additionally, the technology has been credited by professional coaches for significantly contributing to winning sports events, ranging from football championships to National and Olympic judo medals.

Practical Applications

Simply by following my journey from criminalist to author and creator of the patented InnerTalk subliminal technology, it should be clear to you by now that there are a large number of ways subliminal communication can be used to enhance your own personal growth. The only thing left to cover then is how to incorporate subliminal information to benefit you and to counteract the vast amount of negative programming we're all subjected to on a daily basis.

CHAPTER TEN

The Homemade Subliminal Program

InnerTalk technology is the easiest way to create change, and you're welcome to visit the InnerTalk website (**http://www.innertalk.com**) to see the hundreds of programs offered on different subjects. But this book is about what you can do on your own. If you wish to create a customized subliminal program for yourself, then here are some simple instructions. While the InnerTalk technology is patented, this is a technique I've taught to therapists for many years for use in their own practices. It isn't the full InnerTalk technology, as that takes very specialized equipment, but it's still very effective.

Creating an audio subliminal program that works is a relatively simple process, and with the advances in technology these days, it can also be relatively inexpensive. The procedure outlined in this chapter was used in my own early research. This process won't produce commercial-quality audio mastering, but it will provide a usable product.

There are certain advantages to creating your own subliminal property. You should weigh those benefits against professional standards and quality before investing the time or money necessary to produce a personalized subliminal program.

Some of the obvious advantages include a subliminal script that can be uniquely and precisely what you desire. (Be careful here—much bad karma will come from deliberate or exploitive misuse.) Also, you can select whatever music or principal sound carrier you prefer. You may choose the gentle rhythm of a waterfall or ocean background to be used while viewing television or sleeping, or more upbeat music to enjoy as you go about your day. I'm reminded here of a woman who surreptitiously played a program for good study habits with the sound of ocean waves to her teenagers while they viewed television. She reported that within a short time, the kids turned off the TV and moved to their rooms to study. However, whatever the primary carrier you choose, be careful of copyright infringements!

Another advantage is that the voice on the subliminal track can be your own. There's much research suggesting that in many circumstances you'll have a better response with a subliminal program when your own voice is used. (Note: some research suggests that using your own voice may also meet with added resistance.)

Six Steps to Creating a Custom Subliminal Program

The six steps to creating a custom program are these:

1. Select and obtain the equipment.

2. Write and record the script.
3. Select the white sound.
4. Select the principal carrier.
5. Mix the script recording with the white-sound recording.
6. Mix the white-sound/affirmation track with the primary carrier.

1. Select and Obtain the Equipment

These days, advances in technology means that most of us will have all the equipment we need right in our computers. Most sound-mixing software programs will work.

2. Write and Record the Script

Great care needs to be taken when writing and recording the script (or affirmations) that you'll use on your custom program. The fact is that the subconscious mind isn't concerned with sentences. The subconscious cerebration process I mentioned earlier takes place when words are put into the subconscious mind. Like a dice tumbler in Las Vegas, the subconscious just tumbles them all around. Words become separated from each other and their original sentence structure. For this reason, it's absolutely critical that all affirmations used in subliminal communication be positively directed at the desired change. For example, a tapering-off smoking script that said, *I find ten cigarettes a day more than enough for me,* might tumble around and become *more than ten cigarettes.*

It's also important that no aversive approaches be included. Since a known deterioration effect to the subliminal may follow its suspended use, and the result may be that the nonsmoker starts smoking again, it's irresponsible to leave associations about black lungs and smoking in the subconscious, for this creates a psychological predisposition or expectation of lung disease. Aversive therapy was, for the most part, abandoned decades ago, largely due to this type of backlash. As with the iatrogenic (or physician-caused) effect that doctors are careful of, affirmations linking negatives to the stated objective may elicit more harmful results than the desired positive ones.

Subliminal verbalizations should also be first person, such as *I am good* and *I am smart,* as opposed to *You are good,* and *You are smart.* If you think about it, a program designed to build esteem that uses affirmations recorded in the second person (*You are good*) simply can't be effective because the user would feel as though everyone else was good and therefore he or she was . . . not as good?

Another nuance to language is the manner in which we take in information. For example, some of us are primarily visual and therefore "see" data. We think of seeing the problem, or we say, "I see what you mean." Others are kinesthetic, or feeling oriented—we feel instead of see.

Many differences between people can be reduced to arguments over one person saying, "I feel this way," with a response of, "Well, I see it this way." So to some, visual phrasing is more powerful than tactile or auditory. Language in a subliminal script should take these differences into consideration to create vivid, sensory information.

Because the verbal content of subliminals offered in the marketplace is of such great importance, all of the InnerTalk programs come with a published list of the affirmations.

Based on my own research and experience, I also believe that all subliminal programs should also include what I call the "Forgiveness Set":

1. I forgive myself.
2. I forgive all others.
3. I am forgiven.

Another concern regarding the affirmations has nothing to do with the script but rather with the sex of the voice communicating subliminally. As I outlined earlier, some research indicates that certain personality types will respond to one or the other (male or female) in a preferential manner.

Dr. Thomas Budzynski once indicated to me in a telephone conversation that certain feminists had experienced reverse effects from his weight-loss program. That is to say, they went on an eating binge for a few days, but the effects weren't lasting, other than the fact that the women involved ceased using their subliminal audio programs. Budzynski attributes this response to the male voice and the strong resentment held by certain female subjects for male authority figures.

Another alternative for consumers to consider is the dichotic or "whole-brain" programming—presenting a different subliminal message to each hemisphere, which I discussed in Chapter 9. It's generally held that for most right-handed people, the major hemisphere is the left brain, and the minor hemisphere is the right brain. The left hemisphere, then, is usually the discriminate brain; and the right is the indiscriminate. The left is the analytical, the right is the creative, and so forth. It's also generally accepted that the minor hemisphere processes more deeply emotional content and is the repository for unconscious motives behind habits, beliefs, and attitudes.

On my InnerTalk programs, the affirmations are recorded on two channels: on the left channel (to be processed by the right brain) are the authoritarian affirmations (such as *I am good*), while on the right channel (for the left brain) are the permissive affirmations (such as *It's okay to be good*).

The affirmations should then be spoken slowly and meaningfully while they're being recorded. Once recorded, you'll want to serialize the affirmations until they fit the length of music you're using.

3. Select the White Sound

There are lots of sources for white sound these days. If you wish, you can purchase a white-noise generator. Most of these will give you a choice of rain, ocean, or other such sounds. The white noise needs to be a little longer than the affirmations.

4. Select the Principal Carrier

For your homemade subliminal program, music generally works best, although you can remix white sound with white sound if you wish. Most of the InnerTalk programs come with a choice of either music or nature as the primary carrier. Many people like to use the music during the day and the nature at night while they sleep.

You should take care when selecting any music you'll use for several reasons, as research has confirmed the old quotation that "music has charms to soothe a savage breast"—at least certain types of music, that is.

Steven Halpern is one of the leaders in a field often referred to as New Age music. His music has been field tested and demonstrated to relieve anxiety and tension levels, increase learning skills, raise pain thresholds, and more. In his book *Sound Health,* Halpern asserts that music was routinely used in the Soviet Union to raise pain thresholds and thereby minimize the use of pharmaceuticals.[1]

A major difference between New Age and popular music is that in the former, there's no beginning, middle, or end. A person can listen to this music over and over and still be unable to hum along or anticipate the movement.

Another leading musician in this area is Jim Oliver, who has worked with medical professionals for years, measuring major and minor muscle groupings and their responses to different notes, waveform frequencies (such as square wave and sine wave), duration of intonation, and so forth. In a telephone conversation, he reported work with health professionals that was absolutely astounding. He calls the study of music in connection with psychological and physiological responses "synphonics."

I've been so impressed with music by artists such as Steven Halpern, Jim Oliver, and very recently the inspired work of Carla Reed, that I have acquired the rights to use some of them on my InnerTalk programs. In fact, my last book, *I Believe,* comes with a free InnerTalk CD that uses Carla Reed's music!

Sheila Ostrander and Lynn Schroeder, authors of *Superlearning,* a must on anyone's reading list, document the use of baroque music as an essential aspect of the superlearning process. They go to great lengths, listing various classical pieces that produce the desired effects.[2]

Baroque music, usually largo in speed of performance, seems to engender mind entrainment, thereby slowing down brain-wave patterns. This speed reduction enhances the learning process. The slower brain-wave patterns combine with timed repetition of material to produce incredible increases in learning. Repetitive material delivered in this manner is reminiscent of the therapeutic repetition of suggestions in hypnosis.

For that matter, the same sort of repetition takes place in the media. As Dr. Roy Udolf points out, the repetition of a message with perhaps a slight change, such as an omission of the concluding portion of an often-viewed ad, is especially effective.[3] Perhaps one reason for the effectiveness is the Zeigarnik effect, which is produced by the omission of the closure expected by the audience and results in increased memory retention.

Advertisers and the entertainment industry have long appreciated the effect music has on the audience. Among other things, it can excite us, motivate us, raise deep emotion, and build terror. According to scientist, musician, and inventor Manfred Clynes, studies clearly suggest that basic neurological forms or patterns correspond to emotional sets. Clynes refers to this correspondence as "sentics" (from *essentic forms*). Using a computer to play standard notes directly proportional to the intensity and duration associated with different emotions, Clynes discovered that listeners experienced the emotion.[4]

5. Mix the Script Recording with the White Sound Recording

Once you have the recordings of the music, white sound, and affirmations, they should all be imported into the sound software you've chosen to use. Then you're ready to start mixing!

First you'll layer the white sound with the recorded affirmation. Adjust the mixing volume so that you can just perceive the spoken words when they're mixed with the white sound. You should allow 30 to 60 seconds of lead in, where you have just the white sound before starting the affirmations.

6. Mix the White-Sound/Affirmation Track with the Primary Carrier

Once this mix is complete, then remix it with your music (or secondary white sound). Bring in the music (or secondary white sound) a few seconds after the start of the first mix. You should find that when the music starts, the brain is too distracted to hear the affirmations anymore.

Using Your Subliminal Program

Whether you've chosen to create your own custom subliminal program or to purchase one, using the program is very easy. It can be played while you're utilizing the self-hypnosis techniques covered in the earlier section of this book to enhance the hypnotic effect or to assist you in recovering information while in hypnosis, or they can simply be running in the background as you go about your day. I like to put them on my smartphone and play them everywhere I go. Subliminal programs can also be played all night long while you sleep. There are, of course, some obvious contraindications you should take into consideration. You clearly wouldn't use a *Sleep Soundly* program while driving, just as you wouldn't want to use a *High Energy* program while sleeping. But apart from these kinds of situations and concerns, subliminal communication really is a tool you can use virtually anywhere and at anytime. That said, do exercise wisdom and discretion when writing your own scripts.

AFTERWORD

My intention with this book was to share with you the two technologies that I believe are the most flexible, affordable, and powerful for empowering your every ambition. We began with a journey designed to flesh out the power of the mind and provide specific tools and techniques to access the vast reservoir of nearly unlimited potential that rests within each of us. I hope that by now you've glimpsed the awesome possibilities that lie ahead of you.

I've studied the mind and its role in human endeavors for most of my life. I'm absolutely convinced that belief in ourselves is the formula for success in all walks of life. Contrast that to the almost 24/7 bombardment of information designed to inform us all of our deficiencies, and it's easy to understand why perfectly capable people fall short of their goals, ambitions, and abilities.

Today, according to the A. C. Nielsen Company, the average American watches more than four hours of television every day.[1] That's more than 52 days of nonstop TV watching each year. Cumulatively, that means that by the age of 65, the average American will have spent nearly nine years watching television. Furthermore, most estimates find that by the time young people are 18 years old, they've seen some 200,000 commercials. Now this is TV alone, not the Internet, radio, billboards, and so on—

just television. The purpose of all of these commercials is to convince you that you're deficient in some way. You're too fat; your complexion is poor; your hair isn't soft and full enough; or it's your makeup, body, or belongings. Think of the commercials and understand that in order to buy products, you must feel you need them. It's as simple as this: you can't sell a life vest to someone who has no fear of drowning.

Add to this the organic way in which most of us are raised, where our parents, peers, and others tell us things such as, "You're not smart enough, you're not old enough, you're too heavy, you're not attractive enough, you're not talented enough, and you'll never amount to anything," and on and on, ad absurdum. What would we expect if we programmed a computer with this negativity? Unfortunately, our personal outcome often isn't much different than the negative results a computer would kick out. Changing this programming is our best chance to begin to realize our genuine potential.

To that end, I wish you the cornucopia of joy and satisfaction that should be and is yours by birthright if you but learn to truly accept and believe in yourself! The technologies you've just learned will assist you in your journey of honest self-actualization.

Be blessed, and thank you for the read,
Eldon

APPENDIX

Affirmations

Following are the subliminal affirmations used on the accompanying audio download. You may also download the corresponding InnerTalk program by going to **http://www.eldontaylor.com/HypnosisAndSubliminal**.

Hypnosis is natural.
I enjoy hypnosis.
Self-hypnosis is fun.
Self-hypnosis is empowering.
I relax.
I relax easily.
I enter hypnosis easily.
I let go.
I allow.
The quietness of Spirit fills me.
I am calm.
I am comfortable.

I allow myself to go deeply into self-hypnosis.
I enter self-hypnosis easily.
My body relaxes.
It's easy.
It's natural.
I just let go and allow.
I am safe.
I am secure.
I am in control.
I choose to go into hypnosis.
I choose to let go and allow.
I choose to relax.
I choose to go deeply into self-hypnosis.
My mind is powerful.
My mental states are keen.
I am powerful.
I am capable.
I am good.
I enjoy life.
I love living.
I am grateful.
I go deeply into self-hypnosis easily.
I use hypnotic techniques to improve.
I close my eyes and go deeply.

I think, *Relax* in my special way and go deep into self-hypnosis.
I choose when to use self-hypnosis.
I close my eyes, think, *Relax,* and go deeply.
I am wise.
I am intelligent.
I am aware.
I like self-hypnosis.
I keep a record of what I learn in self-hypnosis.
I remember easily.
I improve every day.
Every day in every way, I improve.
Life is fun.
Life is a miracle.
I am a miracle.
I forgive myself.
I forgive all others.
I am forgiven.

Symbiotic messages are included.

AUDIO DOWNLOAD INSTRUCTIONS

Thank you for purchasing *Self-Hypnosis and Subliminal Technology* by Eldon Taylor. This product includes a free download! To access this bonus content, please visit www.hayhouse.com/download and enter the Product ID and Download Code as they appear below.

Product ID: 6750
Download Code: Audio

For further assistance, please contact Hay House Customer Care by phone: US (800) 654-5126 or INTL CC+(760) 431-7695 or visit www.hayhouse.com/contact.

Thank you again for your Hay House purchase. Enjoy!

Hay House, Inc. • P.O. Box 5100 • Carlsbad, CA 92018 • (800) 654-5126

Caution: This audio program features meditation/visualization exercises that render it inappropriate for use while driving or operating heavy machinery.

Publisher's note: Hay House products are intended to be powerful, inspirational, and life-changing tools for personal growth and healing. They are not intended as a substitute for medical care. Please use this audio program under the supervision of your care provider. Neither the author nor Hay House, Inc., assumes any responsibility for your improper use of this product.

AUDIO DOWNLOAD TRACKS

1. Progressive Relaxation
2. Double-Bind Induction
3. Using Affirmations in Hypnosis
4. Power Imaging
5. The Oceanic Experience
6. Out-of-Body Awareness

ENDNOTES

Chapter 2

1. Rossi, E. 2004. "Art, beauty and truth: The psychosocial genomics of consciousness, dreams, and brain growth in psychotherapy." *Annals of the American Psychotherapy Association*, 7, 10–17.

2. Ibid.

3. Ibid.

4. Taylor, E. 2009. *Mind Programming: From Persuasion and Brainwashing to Self Help and Practical Metaphysics*. Carlsbad, Calif.: Hay House, Inc.

5. Nelson, J. 1987. *The Perfect Machine: TV in the Nuclear Age*. Ontario, Canada: Dec Book Distribution.

6. Cialdini, R. B. 1992. *Influence: Science and Practice*. New York: Harper Collins.

7. Ibid.

8. Locke, S., and Colligan, D. 1986. *The Healer Within: The New Medicine of Mind and Body*. New York: E. P. Dutton.

9. Talbot, M. 1991. *The Holographic Universe*. New York: Harper Perennial.

10. Putnam, F. 1987. "Psychoneuroimmunology." *Noetic Sciences*, 4:4.

11. Visintaines, M. 1982. "Immune System Suppressed?—Cancer Linked to Helplessness." *Brain Mind Bulletin*, vol. 7, no. 11B. Originally reported in *Science* (216: 437–440).

12. Williams, R. 1989. "Trusting Hearts Last Longer: Hostility May Be a Type of Toxin." *Brain Mind Bulletin*, vol. 14, no. 6G.

13. Eysenck, H. J. 1989. "Personality Predicts Early Death." *Brain Mind Bulletin*, vol. 14, no. 6B. Also published as "Personality, Stress and Cancer: Prediction and Prophylaxis." *British Journal of Medical Psychology*, 61:57–75.

14. Stanwyk, D. and Anson, C. 1986. "Personality Tied to Clusters of Disease." *Brain Mind Bulletin*, vol. 11, no. 16F.

15. De La Pena, A. 1986. "Boredom, Understimulation May Cause Disease." *Brain Mind Bulletin*, vol. 11, no. 11G.

16. Goodkin, K.; Antoni, M. H.; Sevin, B.; and Fox, B. H. 1993. "A partially testable, predictive model of psychosocial factors in the etiology of cervical cancer i. Biological, psychological and social aspects." *Psycho-Oncology*, vol 2, issue 2, pages 79–98.

17. Van Praag, H. M. 1977. "Cancer, Alcohol and Pot Psychosis." *Brain Mind Bulletin*, vol. 2, no. 4d. Originally reported in *Medical Journal of Australia*, 2:159–163.

18. Rossi, E. 1986. *The Psychobiology of Mind-Body Healing: New Concepts of Therapeutic Hypnosis*. New York: W. W. Norton.

19. Cohen, S. 1991. "Emotional Stress Linked To Common Cold." *Science News*, 140, no.9:132.

20. Kiecolt-Glaser, J. K.; Fisher, L. D.; Ogrocki, P.; Stout, J. C.; Speicher, C. E.; and Glaser, R. 1987. "Marital Quality, Marital Disruption, and Immune Function." *Psychosomatic Medicine*, vol. 49, no. 1.

21. Solomon, G. 1988. "Solomon Charts Mind-Body Communication Model." *Brain Mind Bulletin*, vol. 13, no. 8G.

22. Melnechuk, T. 1984. "Psychoimmunology: For Each State of Mind, A State of Body?" *Brain Mind Bulletin*, vol. 10, no. 2B.

23. Locke, S., and Colligan, D. 1986. *The Healer Within: The New Medicine of Mind and Body*. New York: E. P. Dutton.

24. Taylor, E., 1990. "The Effect of Subliminal Auditory Stimuli in a Surgical Setting Involving Anesthetic Requirements." St. John's University, LA. 1990.

25. Tayor, E. 1991. Personal communication. June 26, 1991.

26. Mutke, P. 1971. "Mental Techniques for Breast Development." Presentation to the Department of Neuropsychiatry, UCLA. Feb. 28.

27. Staff. 2003. "Natural Breast Enlargement Through Mind Training." *What Medicine*, Summer 2003.

28. Taylor, E. 2012. *I Believe: When What You Believe Matters!* Carlsbad, Calif.: Hay House, Inc.

29. Rossi, E. 1993. *Psychobiology of Mind Body Healing: New Concepts of Therapeutic Healing*. New York: W. W. Norton and Company.

30. Kyodo News International. 2001. *Mass Hysteria hits Malaysian School*. **http://findarticles.com/p/articles/mi_m0WDP/is_2001_July_16/ai_77057810/.**

31. Talbot, M. 1991. *The Holographic Universe*. New York: Harper Perennial.

32. Radin, D. 2006. *Entangled Minds*. New York: Pocket Paraview.

33. Targ, R. 2005. *Mind Reach: Scientists Look at Psychic Abilities*. Newburyport, Mass.: Hampton Roads Pub.

34. Massey, H. 2009. *Science Of The Lost Symbol.* **http://www.scienceofthelostsymbol.com/Human-Influence-on-Living-and-Non-living-Systems.html.**

35. Backster, C. 2003. *Primary Perception: Biocommunication with Plants, Living Foods, and Human Cells.* Anza, Calif.: White Rose Millennium Press.

36. Puthoff, H. E., and Fontes, R. 1975. "Organic Biofield Sensor." *Electronics and Bioengineering Laboratory Stanford Research Institute*–S.R.I Project 3194 (Task 3).

37. Tompkins, P., and Bird, C. 1989. *The Secret Life of Plants.* New York, NY: Harper Perennial.

38. Taylor, E. 1992. *Wellness: Just a State of Mind?* Medical Lake, Wash.: R. K. Books.

39. Cromie, W. J. 2002. "Meditation changes temperatures: Mind controls body in extreme experiments." *Harvard University Gazette.* **http://news.harvard.edu/gazette/2002/04.18/09-tummo.html.**

40. Romains, J. 1960. "CIA Study on Brainwashing."

41. Taylor, E. 2011. *What If? The Challenge of Self-Realization.* Carlsbad, Calif.: Hay House, Inc.

Chapter 3

1. Krasner, A. M. 1990. *The Wizard Within.* Irvine, Calif.: ABH Press.

2. Udolf, R. 1981. *Handbook of Hypnosis for Professionals.* New York: Van Norstrand Reinhold Company.

3. Locke, S., and Colligan, D. 1986. *The Healer Within: The New Medicine of Mind and Body.* New York: E. P. Dutton.

4. Ibid.

5. Radin, D., and Nelson, R. 2000. *Meta-analysis of mind-matter interaction experiments: 1959 to 2000.* Boundary Institute, Los Altos, California, Princeton Engineering Anomalies Research, Princeton University.

Chapter 5

1. Nelson, J. 1987. *The Perfect Machine: TV in the Nuclear Age*. Ontario, Canada: Dec Book Distribution.

2. Ostrander, S. and Schroeder, L. 1997. *Superlearning 2000: New Triple Fast Ways You Can Learn, Earn, and Succeed in the 21st Century.* New York: Dell Publishing.

3. Moine, D., and Lloyd, K. 1990. *Unlimited Selling Power: How to Master Hypnotic Selling Skills.* New York: Prentice Hall Press.

4. Taylor, E. 2009. *Mind Programming: From Persuasion and Brainwashing to Self Help and Practical Metaphysics.* Carlsbad, Calif.: Hay House, Inc.

5. Nelson, J. 1987. *The Perfect Machine: TV in the Nuclear Age*. Ontario, Canada: Dec Book Distribution.

6. Sacks, O. 1999. *Awakenings*. New York: Vintage Press.

7. Maltz, M. 1969. *Psycho-Cybernetics*. New York: Pocket Books.

Chapter 8

1. Packard, V. 1957. *The Hidden Persuaders.* New York: Pocket Book.

2. Key, W. B. 1976. *Media Sexploitation.* New York: Signet.
—— 1980. *The Clam-Plate Orgy.* New York: Signet.
—— 1994. *Subliminal Seduction.* New York: Signet.

3. Wolman, B. B. 1973. *Handbook of General Psychology*. Englewood Cliffs, N.J.: Prentice-Hall.

4. Dunham, W. R. 1984. *The Science of Vital Force*. Boston, Mass.: Damrell and Upham.

5. Wolman, B. B. 1973. *Handbook of General Psychology*. Englewood Cliffs, N.J.: Prentice-Hall.

6. Ibid.

7. Ibid.

8. Ibid.

9. Dixon, N. 1981. *Preconscious Processing*. New York: John Wiley & Sons.

10. U.S. House of Representatives. 1984. Subliminal Communication Technology: Committee on Science and Technology. Honolulu, Hawaii: University Press of the Pacific.

11. Greenwald, A. G.; Spangenberg, E. R.; Pratkanis, A. R.; and Eskenazi, J. 1991. "Double-Blind Tests Of Subliminal Self-Help Audio Tapes." *Psychological Science* 2: 119–122.

12. Whitehead, J. E. 1991. "Vance, J., Vance, E.J.R., Vance, P., Robertson, A., -vs- Judas Priest, CBS et al." Case No. 86–5844 and 86–3939. Dept. No. 1. Judicial District Court of the State of Nevada in and for the County of Washoe.

13. Choi, C. 2007. "Subliminal Messages Fuel Anxiety." Live Science. **http://www.livescience.com/health/070802_micro_expressions.html.**

14. Motluk, A. 2006. "Subliminal Advertising May Work After All." *New Scientist,* 2549, 16.

15. CBC News. 2007. "Ontario removes video slot machines flashing winning images." CBCNEWS.CA, Feb. 26. **http://www.cbc.ca/canada/story/2007/02/25/video-lottery.html.**

16. Nauert, R. 2007. "The Influence of Subliminal Messages." Psych Central. **http://psychcentral.com/news/2007/12/27/the-influence-of-subliminalmessages/1712.html.**

17. Claburn, T. 2008. "Apple's Logo Makes You More Creative Than IBM's." *Information Week,* March 19. **http://www.informationweek.com/news/internet/showArticle.jhtml?articleID=206904786.**

18. BBC News. 2007. "Subliminal images impact on brain." March 9. **http://news.bbc.co.uk/2/hi/health/6427951.stm.**

19. Spiering, M.; Everaerd, W.; Karsdrop, P. and Both, S. 2006. "NonconsciousProcess of Sexual Information: A Generalization to Women." *The Journal of Sex Research,* 43.

20. Ibid.

21. Ferraro, R.; Bettman, J. R.; and Chartrand, T. 2009. "The Power of Strangers: The Effect of Incidental Consumer-Brand Encounters on Brand Choice." *Journal of Consumer Research:* February 2009.

22. Lee, J. 2008. "Ten investigated on split-second ads." *The Sidney Morning Herald,* Feb. 21, 2008.

23. Perkins, S. 2003. "Dirty Rats: Campaign Ad May Have Swayed Voters Subliminally." Science News, 163/8, pp. 116–117.

Chapter 9

1. Kappas, J. 1999. *Professional Hypnotism Manual: Introducing Physical And Emotional Suggestibility And Sexuality.* Tarzana, Calif.: Panorama Pub. Co.

2. Gonzalez, J. S. H. 1998. Unpublished Report.

3. Sraon, H. S. 1997. "Weight Loss Study Produces Early Success," *Oxygram*, vol. 13, Issue II, Dec. 1997.

4. Shuman, M. P. 1997. Unpublished report: General Director Special Programs of Instruction.

5. Plante, T. G.; Doan, B. T.; DiGregorio, M.P.; and Manuel, G. M. 1993. "The Influence of Aerobic Exercise and Relaxation Training on Coping With Test-Taking Anxiety." Children's Health Council/Stanford University, Calif.

6. Roche, K. 1993. "The Effects of Auditory Subliminal Messages on the Behavior of Attention Deficit Disordered Children." University of Phoenix, Ariz.

7. Ashley, D. 1993. "The Effect of Subliminally-Presented Reinforcing Stimuli on Factual Material." University of Southern California, Calif.

8. Pelka, R. 1991. "Application of Subliminal Therapy to Over Weight Subjects." Armed Forces University Munich, Germany.

9. Taylor, E. 1992. "Longitudinal Study: Cancer Remission." Progressive Awareness Research, Wash.

10. Isaacs, J. 1991. Unpublished report. "The Other 90%," Calif.

11. Kruse, P. et. al. 1991. "Suggestion and Perceptual Instability: Auditory Subliminal Influences." Bremen University, Germany.

12. Galbraith, P. and Barton, B. 1990. "Subliminal Relaxation: Myth or Method." Weber State University, Utah.

13. Reid, J. 1990. "Free of Depression Subliminal Tape Study." Colorado State University, Colo.

14. Taylor, E. 1990. "The Effect of Subliminal Auditory Stimuli in a Surgical Setting Involving Anesthetic Requirements." Progressive Awareness Research, Wash.

15. Taylor, E.; McCusker, C.; and Liston, L. 1986. "A Study of the Effects of Subliminal Communication on Inmates at the Utah State Prison." *Subliminal Communication.* Medical Lake, Wash: R. K. Books.

Chapter 10

1. Halpern, S. 1985. *Sound Health Sound Health: The Music and Sounds That Make Us Whole.* New York: Harper Collins.

2. Ostrander, S., and Schroeder, L. 1997. Superlearning 2000: *New Triple-Fast Ways You Can Learn, Earn, and Succeed in the 21st Century.* New York: Dell Publishing.

3. Udolf, R. 1981. *Handbook of Hypnosis for Professionals.* New York: Van Norstrand Reinhold Company.

4. Clynes, M. 1978. *Sentics: The Touch of the Emotions.* New York: Anchor Press/ Doubleday.

Afterword

1. 1. Herr, N. *Television and Health.* **http://www.csun.edu/science/health/docs/ tv&health.html#tv_stats.**

ABOUT THE AUTHOR

Eldon Taylor is an award-winning, *New York Times* best-selling author of more than 300 books and audio and video programs. He's the inventor of the patented InnerTalk® technology and the founder and president of Progressive Awareness Research. He has been called a "master of the mind" and has appeared as an expert witness on both hypnosis and subliminal communication.

Eldon was a practicing criminalist conducting investigations and lie-detection examinations for many years. He's listed in more than a dozen Who's Who publications, including *Who's Who of Intellectuals* and *Who's Who in Science and Engineering.* He's a Fellow in the American Psychotherapy Association and an internationally sought-after speaker. His books and audio-video materials have been translated into more than a dozen languages and have sold millions worldwide.

Eldon is the host of the popular radio show *Provocative Enlightenment.* He has interviewed some of the most interesting people on the planet. His shows are provocative and always fresh in both their perspective and the exchanges.

To Learn More about Eldon Taylor

If you've enjoyed this book and would like to learn more about tools to help you become the person you were meant to be, visit Eldon's website: **http://www.eldontaylor.com**.

If you're interested in gaining more control over your self-talk and your own inner beliefs, you may wish to try Eldon's patented audio technology, known as InnerTalk®. Independent researchers have repeatedly proved that InnerTalk is effective at changing thoughts and thereby influencing behavior in a variety of areas affecting our daily lives.

You may download free samples of InnerTalk and find a large selection of self-improvement products by going to **http://www.innertalk.com**.

To be informed about Eldon's latest research and work and to hear about special offers on Eldon's books and audio products, please subscribe to his free e-newsletter by going to **http://www.eldontaylor.com**. You may also request a free catalog online, by calling 800-964-3551, or by writing to Progressive Awareness Research, Inc., P.O. Box 1139, Medical Lake, WA, 99022.

Licensed InnerTalk Distribution

USA
Progressive Awareness Research, Inc.
PO Box 1139
Medical Lake, WA 99022
U.S.A.
1-800-964-3551
1-509-299-3377
www.innertalk.com

UK
Kiki Ltd.
Unit 4, Aylsham Business Estate
Shepheards Close
Aylsham
Norwich
NR11 6SZ
Tel: 01263 738 663
http://www.kiki-health.co.uk/products_innertalk.asp

Germany
Axent Verlag
Steinerne Furt 78
86167 Augsburg

Germany
011 49 821 70 5011
www.axent-verlag.de

Malaysia/Singapore/Brunei
InnerTalk Sdn Bhd
2–2 Jalan Pju 8/5E, Perdana Bus. Cntr.
Bandar Damansara Perdana,
47820 Petaling Jaya
Selangor, Malaysia
011 60 37 729 4745
www.innertalk.com.my

Taiwan and China
Easy MindOpen
3F, No. 257, Ho-Ping East Rd. Sec. 2
Taipei, Taiwan, R.O.C
011 886 (227) 010–468(1)
www.iamone.com.tw

Distribution Inquiries

For information about distributing InnerTalk programs, either internationally or domestically, please contact:

Progressive Awareness Research, Inc.
PO Box 1139
Medical Lake, WA 99022
1-800-964-3551
1-509-299-3377
www.innertalk.com

Hay House Titles of Related Interest

YOU CAN HEAL YOUR LIFE, the movie,
starring Louise L. Hay & Friends
(available as an online streaming video)
www.hayhouse.com/louise-movie

THE SHIFT, the movie,
starring Dr. Wayne W. Dyer
(available as an online streaming video)
www.hayhouse.com/the-shift-movie

✧✧

AWAKENING THE LUMINOUS MIND: Tibetan Meditation for Inner Peace and Joy, by Tenzin Wangyal Rinpoche

EUFEELING!: The Art of Creating Inner Peace and Outer Prosperity, by Dr. Frank J. Kinslow

THE JOURNEY TO THE SACRED GARDEN: A Guide to Traveling in the Spiritual Realms, by Hank Wesselman, Ph.D.

NO STORM LASTS FOREVER: Transforming Suffering into Insight, by Dr. Terry A. Gordon

QUEST: A Guide for Creating Your Own Vision Quest, by Denise Linn and Meadow Linn

SECRETS OF MEDITATION: A Practical Guide to Inner Peace and Personal Transformation, by davidji

✧✧

HAY HOUSE

HAY HOUSE INDIA

Look within

Join the conversation about latest products, events, exclusive offers, contests, giveaways and more.

Hay House India

@HayHouseIndia

@HayHouseIndia

HayHouse.co.in

We'd love to hear from you!